77-2686

DIALOGUE ON WORLD OIL

A conference sponsored by the
American Enterprise Institute's
National Energy Project

THE AEI
NATIONAL ENERGY PROJECT

The American Enterprise Institute's
National Energy Project was established in early 1974
to examine the broad array of issues
affecting U.S. energy demands and supplies.
The project will commission research into all important
ramifications of the energy problem—economic
and political, domestic and international, private
and public—and will present the results
in studies such as this one.
In addition it will sponsor symposia, debates, conferences,
and workshops, some of which will be televised.

The project is chaired by Melvin R. Laird,
former congressman, secretary of defense,
and domestic counsellor to the President,
and now senior counsellor of *Reader's Digest*.
An advisory council, representing a wide range of
energy-related viewpoints, has been appointed.
The project director is Professor Edward J. Mitchell
of the University of Michigan.

Views expressed are those of the authors
and do not necessarily reflect the views of
either the advisory council and others associated with
the project or of the advisory panels,
staff, officers, and trustees of AEI.

DIALOGUE ON WORLD OIL

Proceedings of a Conference on World Oil

Edited by Edward J. Mitchell
With a foreword by Melvin R. Laird

American Enterprise Institute for Public Policy Research
Washington, D. C.

ISBN 0-8447-2059-3 (Paper)
ISBN 0-8447-2060-7 (Cloth)

Library of Congress Catalog Card No. 74-29419

Printed in the United States of America

MAJOR CONTRIBUTORS

George Ball
Senior Partner, Lehman Brothers

Alan Greenspan
Chairman, Council of Economic Advisers

Hendrik Houthakker
Professor of Economics, Harvard University

Melvin R. Laird
Senior Counsellor, *Reader's Digest*
Chairman, American Enterprise Institute's
National Energy Project

George Lenczowski
Professor of Political Science
University of California, Berkeley

Henry M. Jackson
United States Senator, Washington

Donald S. Macdonald
Minister of Energy, Mines and Resources, Canada

Philip E. Ruppe
United States Congressman, Michigan

John Sawhill
.Administrator, Federal Energy Administration

Herbert Stein
A. Willis Robertson Professor of Economics
University of Virginia

Sheikh Ahmed Zaki Yamani
Minister of Petroleum and Mineral Resources
Saudi Arabia

FOREWORD

In this difficult and challenging decade, the most pervasive issue to be resolved by our economic and political institutions is that of the supply of and demand for the basic ingredient of modern industrial society: energy. In order to help in the vital task of informing the public of the major energy-policy issues and to stimulate original thinking and analysis in this area, I agreed to serve as chairman of the National Energy Project—a nonpartisan, nonprofit undertaking of the American Enterprise Institute for Public Policy Research.

We are proud of the work of the project to date—of the published studies, academic research, and public debates on a wide variety of energy policy issues—but I believe that this conference on world oil problems best epitomizes our efforts. Oil is the lynch pin of the present world energy market. Its price and availability are the central components of the present world fuel mosaic.

To discuss both the economic and political considerations underlying the world oil market, the National Energy Project brought together in Washington an unprecedented spectrum of those interested in and knowledgeable of energy affairs—economists, U.S. government leaders from both the Congress and the executive branch, oil industry spokesmen, representatives from oil-exporting countries around the globe, state and local government officials, environmentalists, and scientists. Each participant brought a unique perspective, and I believe we each took away from this conference a broadened understanding of the others' points of view.

Even though the complexity of these problems is matched only by their importance, the underlying conclusion of this conference is the irreplaceable need for interchange of ideas and perspectives. The most dangerous shortage of all is a shortage of international understanding.

I am glad that we can share the excitement of this conference through this publication. I hope that you will be challenged to rethink these cardinal policy questions with the participants.

MELVIN R. LAIRD

11 November 1974

CONTENTS

INTRODUCTION

Edward J. Mitchell

In October 1973, Arab oil-exporting nations sharply reduced their production of crude oil and imposed a complete embargo on exports to the United States. Subsequently, crude oil prices in the Arab Persian Gulf rose fourfold and have sustained that level since. The problems these events have created hardly need recounting. Today oil-consuming nations face stiffly higher prices, the threat of future cutbacks or embargoes, and, in some cases, a financial condition that can only be labeled critical.

On the first anniversary of the embargo and price escalation the AEI National Energy Project sponsored a conference on world oil problems for the purpose of bringing together experts to analyze and discuss the issues growing out of these events. The conference was held at the American Enterprise Institute in Washington on 3–4 October 1974. This volume presents an edited version of the conference proceedings.

The conference was unique in many respects. It offered a forum for discussion of world oil problems among representatives of oil-producing and oil-consuming nations. It brought together members of different disciplines—economics and political science—and different interests—oil company executives, environmentalists, and consumerists. All this was done on a scale small enough to encourage candid exchanges of views and extended discussions of important topics.

In a conference like this, the quality of the participants is crucial. We were fortunate in having a stellar cast. We began on the morning of 3 October with a paper on the world oil market by Hendrik Houthakker of Harvard University, which stimulated a great deal of discussion on the comparative roles of politics and economics in determining world oil prices.

At luncheon Donald Macdonald, Canadian minister of energy, mines and resources, examined Canadian energy problems as a microcosm of the world energy situation.

The afternoon discussion focused on a paper by Professor George Lenczowski of the University of California at Berkeley on the politics of world oil. During this session representatives of oil-exporting countries made strong appeals for a meeting with oil-consuming nations for the purpose of resolving some of the problems created by world oil costs.

1

At dinner that evening Alan Greenspan, chairman of the President's Council of Economic Advisers, answered questions from the press and others on the impact of the world oil problem on the American economy.

A televised panel discussion and question and answer session was the highlight of the conference's second day. Six prominent and knowledgeable participants comprised the panel: George Ball, former under secretary of state and now a partner in Lehman Brothers and a member of the National Energy Project's Advisory Council, Donald S. Macdonald, Canadian energy minister, Sheikh Ahmed Zaki Yamani, Saudi Arabia's minister of petroleum and mineral resources, Henry M. Jackson, United States senator from Washington, and John W. Sawhill, federal energy administrator at the time of the conference. The panel chairman was Melvin R. Laird, former secretary of defense and chairman of the National Energy Project. After an hour-long discussion among the six panelists, the other conference participants joined in a wide-ranging discussion of all aspects of world oil.

One of the major features of the conference was the beginning of a dialogue between the major producers and consumers of petroleum. This was pointed out most clearly by one of the conference participants, Dr. Reza Fallah, of the National Iranian Oil Company:

> . . . to the best of my knowledge, this is the only round table where I see two representatives of producing governments present—Ambassador Al-Sabah and Ambassador Zahedi. Don't you agree that this sort of dialogue and the coordination and cooperation between the two sides, rather than confrontation, which has been the order of the day, would do a great deal in order for both sides to understand, realize and appreciate each other's problems?

The production and dissemination of such dialogues on all aspects of the energy issue is the aim of the National Energy Project.

PART ONE

Supply, Demand, and the Price of Oil

Professor Hendrik Houthakker opened this session of the conference by asserting that the 1973–74 rise in oil prices, like the price rise in other basic commodities, reflected short-term worldwide demand conditions. He predicted the price of oil would fall because a lower price would maximize long-run Arab revenue.

SUPPLY, DEMAND, AND THE PRICE OF OIL

HERBERT STEIN, University of Virginia, session chairman: Paul McCracken was to have been the chairman of this session. He has been delayed for a couple of hours preparing one of those seven-point programs for finally stabilizing the American economy that the government produces every few months. Since I am no longer in that business, I will substitute for him.

I was at a meeting in New York yesterday, where I got into a discussion of the process of U.S. government policy making. One of the participants, who had been a government official at the same time as I, remarked that in about three years of attending interagency meetings, whether the subject was transportation or agriculture or trade or energy, the most influential person in the meeting was always Hendrik Houthakker of the President's Council of Economic Advisers.

I explained that that was because Professor Houthakker was always the most informed person, and even in the federal government, being the most informed person attracts a certain amount of influence. Also, Henk has an unusual capacity for marrying economic analysis and quantitative measurement, and he has deep institutional knowledge of both the economic and political spheres.

Henk began his excursion into the field of energy around 1969, when the U.S. government began studying the oil import question. He participated on behalf of the Council of Economic Advisers in that study, which was chaired by George Shultz, and he has remained a leading, original, and uninhibited thinker about this question ever since. He has written some very useful things, and I am sure has some useful things to say today about the economics of oil.

HENDRIK HOUTHAKKER, Harvard University: Thank you very much, Herb, for your kind introduction.

As you pointed out, my interest in energy goes back to the Oil Import Task Force of 1969. It was a very illuminating exercise, but it left me with a feeling that a great deal more is needed before we can talk about a coherent energy policy. After I went back to Harvard, I decided to do some research on the subject.

My own background in energy is neither very deep nor longstanding, and I have, therefore, drawn on other areas in which I do have somewhat greater experience, in particular, commodity markets, in which I have been interested for many years.

To me the oil market is basically a commodity market, and it should be analyzed to a large extent with the procedures that are appropriate for commodity markets. There are differences between the oil market and other commodity markets. The most important difference is that in the petroleum market there is no central trading, there is no Chicago Board of Trade or London Metal Exchange. But despite this important difference, there are also important parallels.

In the first place, oil was just one of many commodities whose price took off in 1972 and 1973. Most raw materials took off earlier than oil, but that is due, in large part, to the fact that they are centrally traded. The existence of central markets—which usually are used by speculators—makes it easier for such markets to react to changes in economic conditions; a lot of anticipation goes on in them. Therefore, in 1972 and 1973 we saw a great many commodity markets rise very sharply. The immediate reason why they rose, in many cases at least, was that inventories had run low.

In 1972 and 1973 we had a worldwide boom—something that doesn't happen very often. Usually the various economies of the world are somewhat out of phase with each other, but at that time, perhaps because of improved international cooperation, perhaps for other reasons, all the economies of the world were in a boom situation at the same time, and this exercised strong pressure on raw materials. As a result, inventories ran down and prices in these markets generally went quite high.

Some things went up earlier than others. Wool was one of the first commodities to go up. Its price more than doubled; it is now back to about where it was before the boom. Other commodities have shown somewhat similar movements.

I mention this, in part, because commodity markets have a long history of overshooting. Generally speaking, when there is an excess of demand over supply in a commodity market, the price goes way, way up; the sky seems to be the limit for a few months. At first prices rise continuously; then some hesitation sets in, which usually takes a long time to crystallize in a price decline. Some of the markets that went up very early have already reached this second phase, others have not.

I don't believe that the reasons for this general increase in commodity prices are to be found in the markets themselves. In other words, what we have seen in the last few years is not a commodity inflation. The reasons for the worldwide inflation which is still very much with us, and which started in the commodity markets, are essentially monetary. I believe they have much to do with the gradual breakdown of the Bretton Woods system, and the resulting change in the need for international reserves.

In other words, I don't think what we have at the moment can properly be called a raw-materials or commodity inflation; it just happens that commodity markets are very sensitive to changes in economic conditions. The commodity markets are better thermometers than most other markets, but they are not the cause of the inflationary fever that has gripped the whole world.

6

The oil market also fits into this pattern, but since there is no central market in oil, it took much longer for these things to come to a head. Perhaps as a result of this, the price rise was also much sharper. It was not a gradual rise, because in the oil market there is virtually no mechanism allowing a gradual rise; things generally move by leaps and bounds—as they did this time. So we found after the worldwide boom of 1972–73 had proceeded for a year or so that inventories were low generally. As a result, the consumers were in no position to resist price increases, which in this case were largely imposed by OPEC members. As it happens, OPEC has come to be the principal price-making mechanism in the world petroleum market. Oil companies used to have a large role, but this has gradually eroded for reasons that we can perhaps come back to.

Now, some people in this room undoubtedly know much more about the detailed history of what happened in the fall of 1973 than I do. As an outsider, I can only conjecture. I don't know exactly what role the Middle East war of October 1973 played in the various events. This is, I think, still obscure and probably will remain obscure until various people write their memoirs.

One thing is clear: the embargo which was part of the October war did make a tremendous impact on consumers. The world "panic" is not too strong for what happened in many countries, especially France and Japan. These countries found themselves naked to a threat from which they saw absolutely no way to defend themselves. This, in turn, may have facilitated the decision by the petroleum-producing countries to raise the price by the large amount that they did in December 1973.

Again, I don't want to suggest that I know the exact sequence of events. I do not know to what extent these things had been planned before the outbreak of the war. The fact is that the embargo itself demonstrated the weakness of consumers, and once this had been demonstrated, there was very little that could be done to prevent a large price increase.

The price increase was a very substantial one, larger indeed than those in most commodity markets. However, it is not outside the general range of what happened in those markets. And one can argue that since there is no central trading in oil, the price had remained rather low for some time. That, of course, is a question open to debate.

I draw this parallel with commodity markets in part to suggest that subsequent developments may be similar. After all, in the commodity market it is generally true that what goes up must come down, although not always to the floor we started from. And I believe that something of the same thing is true also in the world oil market. In this respect, I would emphasize the role of low inventories. Inventories were very important in the initial price increase. If there had been normal or even large inventories, the price increase would have been much harder to enforce. But, as it was, it was self-enforcing.

Since the price increase, a number of things have happened. In the first place, there has been a fall in demand. I have seen a figure for Germany estimating consumption this year to be 7 percent below last year. This is a rather startling figure considering that the German economy is at the moment one of the better performing economies. There is still some positive growth in the German economy, something which is not evident in any other country. I have looked at Japanese figures and U.S. figures, and they indicate zero or possibly negative growth. Thus we see there is some demand response to higher prices. How much is not clear at the moment. However, the important thing is that demand is still being kept strong by the desire on the part of many consuming countries to rebuild their inventories. There is under way a determined effort on the part of most consuming countries not to be caught the way they were a year ago, with virtually no inventory. This is a rational policy because, clearly, you cannot bargain if you have to live from hand to mouth, which was the case last year.

In the case of Japan, for instance, there were at the end of this July inventories for crude and fuel oil about 35 percent above the level of July 1973. This reflects a deliberate and continuing effort by Japanese government and business to strengthen their inventory position. The Japanese government, like many other governments, wants to attain inventories to cover at least ninety days' consumption. Japan is still far short of this, and it is having difficulty finding storage space and, perhaps, difficulty finding financing, because building up inventory at present prices and present interest rates is a very expensive proposition. Nevertheless, it is being done.

The United States inventory, of course, has also gone up. About a month ago, inventories were some 20 percent above last year. The same is true in Europe, although I can't supply any figures. What this probably means is that, at the moment, the total demand for petroleum is being inflated by inventory demands to the extent of something like 5 percent; that is, 5 percent of current petroleum purchases is not being consumed currently, but is used to build up stocks. There are also some indications of inventory buildup in producing countries.

However, what matters most is the buildup of inventories in consuming countries, which is still going on. Now, this is important primarily because it will come to a halt at some point. There is no question that the buildup in inventories must end sometime because, in the first place, there are physical and financial limitations. In the second place, the strong demand in which inventory formation plays such a large part is not stable. Somebody is going to ask himself, "What do we do with all this stuff if the price falls?" Therefore, the inventory formation process isn't likely to continue forever.

I have heard plans for building up in the U.S. much larger inventories than ninety days. If any efforts of that kind were made, the inventory-building process would be extended. As it is, my impression is that by sometime late next year most countries of the world will have reached the desired inventories and will not buy anything further.

8

This should be considered against the background of a decline in *current consumption,* apart from inventory demands. I don't believe that this decline has yet come to an end. The world economy is sluggish and, as far as I can see, likely to remain sluggish well into 1975. I don't want to suggest that it is not going to turn around at some point. I believe that the problems which we face at the moment are resolvable, but they are not easy, and they are not going to be solved very quickly. Therefore, the world economy is likely to remain far from buoyant for quite some time.

The demand for petroleum depends quite strongly upon the state of the world economy. In addition, the effect of higher prices has by no means made its full impact felt yet. Studies that have been made of the demand for energy products suggest that there is a considerable difference between the short-run effect and the long-run effect of higher prices. The short-run effect is relatively small and is determined primarily by the stock of energy-using equipment, such as cars and electrical appliances. In the short run, the stock of equipment that uses energy is given, and there is not a great deal that can be done except use less of it. This is the fairly modest short-run effect. In the long run, one can adjust the stock of energy-using equipment to the higher price. That has a more powerful effect, which also takes longer to take place. As an example, take the case of cars: we have already seen a fairly sharp fall-off in the demand for cars and some shift toward smaller cars. This is just one phase of the adjustment of the stock of energy-using equipment to the higher price of energy, an adjustment that is going to continue for some time, for I believe we are just at the beginning of this adjustment to higher energy prices. There are studies that suggest that in the case of petroleum, the adjustment may take something like two or three years.

In the case of electric power, it apparently will take much longer, in part because there is no second-hand market in most electrical equipment. But there is no question that industry and households have found ways of using less energy than they used before.

I don't want to emphasize the so-called conservation aspect of this too much, for I happen to believe that higher prices are a more effective incentive to conservation than exhortations by government officials. But it is possible that such exhortations may have made people aware of the importance of saving energy and thereby also saving some money. In either case, the effect is the same: a continued slow-down and perhaps even a decline in current consumption on top of strong inventory demand that is going to level off probably sometime next year.

Now, what about the supply side, the most difficult sector of the energy market? I say it is the most difficult because economics does not have as much to say about supply as it has about demand, which is relatively simple from an economic point of view.

The supply side is not simple primarily because of the cartelization of supply that has taken place in recent years in the world oil market. The main difference

9

between the commodity markets I talked about earlier and the oil market is not, as I said, that the price of oil has gone up; prices went up in all commodity markets. The main difference is that there is now a cartel in the world oil market which works to keep the price where it is or even raise it, although so far the latter has not happened.

Now, the question of whether the OPEC cartel will hold together is, of course, one of the main questions we face at the moment. Let us first consider the situation where the cartel does hold together, where the cartel succeeds in controlling the world's supply of oil. At what level will it control the price? This, of course, is something about which we can only speculate. There are some calculations one can make and some which I have made, but they are obviously not compelling, because what really matters is the way the cartel members see the situation, not the way an outside economist sees it.

For what it's worth, I have tried to work out what I would do if I were OPEC and had the prospect of receiving all of these billions of dollars. I would—and this may just show my poor education—find a curve relating the price of oil to total revenue.

With a world petroleum model (which I helped develop) that belongs to Data Resources, Incorporated, it is possible to make calculations of this kind: the demand for Middle East and African crude oil as a function of the export tax levied in the Persian Gulf. I believe that the export tax is probably the right factor to consider rather than the posted price, which is more of an accounting figure. The export tax is what has to be paid by buyers in the Persian Gulf over and above production costs—and the production cost, of course, is very low. (The way we calculate it, the production cost varies according to volume. At high volumes it may be twenty-eight cents a barrel, at low volumes ten cents a barrel.) So the important factor is the export tax, and one can calculate for each level of the export tax how many barrels will be sold from the Middle East and Africa (see Table 1).

It turns out that the amount of money is limited by two factors: demand and supply responses in the rest of the world. As a result, there is a maximum revenue that can be obtained by the Middle East/African region at a price, according to my calculations, of somewhere around $6.00 a barrel in 1972 dollars.

Table 1 is, of course, not the last word on the subject. It is an attempt to derive demand in 1980 for Middle Eastern crude from the demand for products and certain other factors such as refining coefficients, transportation costs, and what have you. The table figures are expressed in 1972 dollars, that is, inflation is eliminated from the calculations.

In the table, you find column one lists export tax rates and columns two, three, and four show the crude oil prices in the Middle East and Africa, the U.S. and Europe.

Table 1

CONSEQUENCES OF ALTERNATIVE EXPORT TAX RATES IN THE MIDDLE EAST, 1980

Export Tax Rate (1)	Crude Price in			Crude Production	Product Consumption		Net Crude Exports from			Tax Revenue
	ME&A (2)	USA (3)	Europe (4)	USA (5)	USA (6)	Europe (7)	ME&A (8)	USA (9)	Europe (10)	ME&A (11)
1.00	1.28	2.78	2.28	10.5	19.4	18.9	46.7	−13.2	−19.1	17.0
2.00	2.28	3.78	3.28	11.8	17.5	16.6	37.1	−9.5	−16.3	27.1
3.00	3.28	4.78	4.28	12.9	16.0	15.1	29.9	−6.6	−14.5	32.7
4.00	4.26	5.76	5.26	14.0	14.9	14.1	24.5	−4.2	−13.4	35.8
5.00	5.25	6.75	6.25	14.8	14.0	13.3	20.2	−2.1	−12.5	37.0
6.00	6.23	7.20	7.24	15.3	13.5	12.7	17.7	−1.1	−11.5	38.8
7.00	7.21	8.06	8.21	16.1	12.9	12.2	14.6	−0.3	−10.3	37.3
8.00	8.19	8.66	9.19	16.6	12.5	11.8	12.2	0	−9.7	35.8
9.00	9.16	9.51	10.16	17.3	11.9	11.4	9.7	0.9	−8.8	31.9
10.00	10.13	10.48	11.15	18.0	11.4	11.0	7.3	2.4	−8.4	26.6

Note: "Crude" includes natural gas liquids.

"Products" consist only of gasoline, kerosene, distillate and residual fuel oil.

Columns 1-4: 1972 dollars per barrel.

Columns 5-10: Millions of barrels per day.

Column 11: Billions of 1972 dollars.

11

Up to an export tax rate of $5.00 per barrel the price in the U.S. is just $1.50 more than the price in the Middle East and Africa. This difference represents shipping costs and the U.S. duty.

At higher export tax rates, the U.S. price differential grows smaller, so that at the bottom line, the $10.00 tax line, the price in the United States is only thirty-five cents higher than the Middle East/Africa price.

The table also shows that revenue is maximized at an export tax rate of $6.00 in 1980. This, then, is the main implication of this table: if OPEC holds together, there will be a certain price, depending on the assumptions one makes about supply and demand, that will maximize the export tax revenue.

One may ask, why compare just the Middle East and Africa? Why not include Venezuela and Indonesia, which are important OPEC members? The reason is that there are certain technical problems that prevent this right now, but it will be done at a later state of our calculations. In any case, I think it is fair to say that the Middle East and African countries are the core of OPEC.

Let me say something about oil supplies from other sources, which play an important part in price developments. Primary sources of supply outside the OPEC area are North America, the North Sea, and, possibly, the Communist countries. It should be noted here that in this paper I have not taken into account the Communist countries. The situation there is obscure. China, of course, claims to have substantial production now, and is very anxious to sell to Japan. I have some doubts about the accuracy of the figures that the Chinese mention, but nobody knows for sure. The Soviet Union has made tremendous discoveries in recent years. It is possible that it will have more potential for export than it has had in recent years, but this is most uncertain. The Russians, generally, have a history of looking at exports primarily from a political rather than an economic point of view. Undoubtedly, they could export profitably, but this is not necessarily a sufficient reason for them to export.

We can analyze supply from the North Sea and the United States more easily. It is very clear that the North Sea is a major petroleum province. Calculations have been made by Professor Peter O'Dell at the university in Rotterdam that indicate that by the early 1980s the North Sea will produce 10 to 12 million barrels a day.

There is some question in my mind whether these are realistic figures. Not that I distrust the calculations made by O'Dell, but there are political problems. We just don't know what effect nationalization of the North Sea by the Labor government in Britain would do to the supply. Norway has already earned itself the name of the "blue-eyed Arab" because of its possessive attitude toward the oil found in its waters, and we don't know whether we also have kilted Arabs, too. Therefore, we cannot be sure that the potential of the North Sea will be realized as soon as O'Dell maintains. I mention O'Dell because he predicted this at a time when people did not admit the large extent of the North Sea discovery. His extrapolations have a certain amount of credibility, if only because he saw this coming long before the oil companies were willing to state publicly how much they had found. Nevertheless, we cannot be sure that all this oil will be there by the mid-1980s.

When we come to North America, there are two countries with somewhat different positions. Canada has so far insulated its market—to some extent—by an export tax. Also, the province of Alberta, where most of the oil is located, has a long history of prorationing and of keeping its supply down by all possible means. Therefore, any great optimism about Canada would, I think, be premature. It is possible that, if Canada gets the idea it is missing the boat, it will supply a lot more, but at the moment my impression is that the Canadians are playing this for all it is worth, as would most other people.

Supply and demand controls are not quite as common in the United States. We have a petroleum industry that is more competitive than almost any other in the world. It is true that we have the Texas Railroad Commission, but its influence has gradually diminished. I believe there is still a latent threat in the commission, and I would like to see its authority terminated, but it has not been too much of a problem in the last few years.

It is customary to be very pessimistic about the prospects for U.S. production. I do not share this pessimism, and this may just reflect my ignorance. I believe that a great deal more can be produced. In the first place, we have Alaska coming on the scene. We will have some secondary recovery, and we have some other discoveries—which are not earth-shaking, but they add up to a fair amount of oil— in places like Wyoming, Florida, and other parts of the country.

So I am not prepared to write off the United States as a source of additional supply. However, there are a number of problems which I want to mention. The most significant problem we face concerns the Alaskan oil. Alaska will presumably come on stream to a limited extent sometime in 1977, and the full pipeline should be in operation sometime in 1980. There is apparently no market on the West Coast for all the oil from Alaska. The logical place to send it would be Japan. There is still a question about what reaction this would cause domestically, since originally the pipeline was sold with the idea that we needed to resolve our own energy problems. Many people will not be able to see the connection if we sell Alaskan oil to Japan while importing oil on the East Coast.

Thus there is still some problem with Alaska, but I am hopeful that by 1980 we will be getting 2 or 2.5 million barrels a day from sources such as Alaska.

Now, what does this add up to? It means that there will be additional supplies and that OPEC will not benefit from having a price as high as it is now. Therefore, I foresee some reduction in the price of crude in the world market in the not-too-distant future. Last February, I stuck my neck out and said that the price of oil would come down within two years. I still believe that is a good guess. I am not saying it is coming down this year. I think next year is rather more likely, particularly because of what I said about buildup of inventories.

However, there is a long-run aspect to this. The idea here is that the price will not fall because the producing countries will leave the oil in the ground rather than sell it at a lower price. This, to my mind, is not a rational policy. It is most unlikely that the price of oil in the long run will rise. This is true primarily for various technological reasons which are not very important right now, but which will become important after 1985. Nuclear power has had very mixed success so far. The main trouble is not safety, because the safety record of nuclear plants has been very good. In the main, the record has shown operating reliability. However, most nuclear plants are incapable of operating for as long as they should. This is something which I believe will be cured in due course. It is just a technological problem, and once it is cured, nuclear power will be very competitive. And, though it takes time to build nuclear plants, by 1985 we will have enough nuclear power-generating capacity to make a significant difference in petroleum demand. In addition, there are other oil sources, such as shale and tar sands, whose production costs certainly do not exceed six 1972 dollars.

Therefore, since there are huge amounts of shale and tar sands and nuclear fuels, the long-run price of oil is most unlikely to rise at more than the rate of interest.

There have been many new oil discoveries recently, and more are still to come. There has been an explosion in the number of oil provinces around the world: countries like Libya and Nigeria which were not in the market until 1960 are now major factors; the North Sea oil was discovered only seven or eight years ago; and the big Alaskan strike was made in the late 1960s.

All these things contribute to my feeling that there will be more oil in the future, and that it will not be profitable to leave oil in the ground. This supposition leads to the conclusion that it is not rational for OPEC to cut back supply too much. Indeed, it will be to its own interests to aim at a somewhat lower price in the future.

PROFESSOR STEIN: Thank you, Henk. Now we will open up the discussion among the people around the table. Yes?

VERMONT ROYSTER, University of North Carolina: Professor Houthakker, most of your discussion was based on the assumption that the cartel would hold together, but you noted that it might not hold together. I'd like your assessment, given all the factors that you have laid out, of whether or not it is likely that the cartel will hold together.

PROFESSOR HOUTHAKKER: I am glad you reminded me of that, because I did omit the answer to this before. Let me perhaps refer you to Table 1 again, because, in a way, it contains the answer to this question. At the $6.00 export tax rate, according to this calculation here the revenue is $38.8 billion a year in the Middle East and Africa in 1980. At $4.00 the revenue is $35.8 billion. That is only a $3 billion difference. However, looking now at column 8, crude exports from the Middle East and Africa are 17.7 million barrels a day at $6.00, and 24.5 million barrels at $4.00.

What I am saying is that for $3 billion a year, you can hold OPEC together. It would be difficult, I believe, to reduce production enough to obtain the maximum revenue, and there is not much to be gained from doing so. The political strains involved in cutting nearly 7 million barrels a day of OPEC production are probably not worth the $3 billion. So, the answer to your question is that OPEC can stay together if it doesn't try for the last nickel.

REZA FALLAH, National Iranian Oil Company: I am glad that Professor Houthakker treats oil as a commodity, because for years, the producing countries have thought that the Western countries have looked at it only from a political perspective.

Oil is a commodity; that is how we look upon it. It is a commodity which is governed by, among other market forces, supply and demand. And in this particular case, I would like to say that there is another factor in the world price of energy, and it is the replacement value of our crude oil, which will one day be completely exhausted. In addition to supply and demand, this other factor is brought into the picture by OPEC. One day we shall have exhausted our resources, and we shall have to buy back energy from the Western nations. We certainly would like to take just as much as we have received from you while we have been meeting your energy needs.

However, I would like to comment on one of your prophecies, which may be correct but, to my mind, is not very clear. You said that everything that goes up must come down, and that the price of oil will come down. You said it has gone up very rapidly. In fact, there has been a price explosion which brought about this energy crisis. But that was the result of decades of underpricing.

When you say that the price will come down, I would like to ask what price? Because at the moment there are quite a number of prices. There is equity price, which the Iranian contract demands, and that is what we charge for the crude we sell to the West. That price will never come down, because it is already so cheap. Then there are the participation, buy-back, and the "cut-rate" prices. These prices may come down, but I do believe that the price—which is the basic price that the taxpaid-cost issue is about—$8.30, or something like that—cannot stand any reduction, but the other prices may.

PROFESSOR HOUTHAKKER: I am grateful for Dr. Fallah's comments, and I am happy that there is not a great deal of disagreement between us. As he correctly points out, there are many oil prices. This is one reason why the present situation is hard to analyze.

With regard to Dr. Fallah's contention that oil, until recently, has been under-priced: that is not, of course, an economic judgment. It is possible that before the price increase oil was somewhat underpriced. Since there is no central market in oil, the response to changing economic conditions tends to be slow. It may well be that if there had been a futures market in oil, prices would have gone up much earlier.

I don't believe that one can speak of underpricing of oil in the long run, primarily because so much oil has been found. That, I think, is the main reason why the real price of oil fell during the 1960s, and the difference is the reason why the demand accelerated during the 1960s.

The fact that the real price of a commodity falls doesn't mean that it is underpriced. There are many instances of commodities whose real prices have fallen. This depends on conditions of supply and demand. In the case of oil, it so happens that there had been tremendous new discoveries. Now, if the supply of a commodity increases more rapidly than the demand for it, the real price is very likely to go down. To an economist, at least, this is not underpricing.

One could speak of underpricing if there were a cartel on the demand side which exploited the producing countries, and that may conceivably have been true under the various arrangements that existed before 1960 among the "seven sisters." However, whatever may have happened then really isn't very relevant to the present situation. The oil market has been characterized by distortions of various kinds, most of which originated right here in the United States. Our oil import quota program was in force from 1958 to 1973. It was a major distortion in the world market—one for which we are still paying every day because it meant that our expensive oil was exhausted when we could get cheap oil from abroad.

Factors like quotas tended to keep the price of oil up. The calculations of Nordhaus in the Brookings papers, which are certainly controversial, but neverthe-less illuminating, don't suggest that the price of oil was too low in the recent past.

If there hadn't been these major oil discoveries, we would have been in a different market altogether. Having said this, however, I am glad to know that Dr. Fallah does see the possibility of a drop in the buy-back price, which will of course help, too.

As regards the equity price, a lot depends on whether one is talking in real terms or in money terms. The analysis I have given here is in real terms: 1972 dollars. Since 1972 the world price level has probably increased, depending on what index you take, by something like 20 percent. So that a price of $8.30, which you mentioned, would correspond to something like $7.00 in 1972 prices, perhaps a little less. This isn't too far from what my calculations suggest is the price at which OPEC would maximize its revenue.

I believe that ultimately supply and demand will determine price, subject to the anticompetitive arrangements that may exist, and that therefore one cannot say a priori that a certain current price will hold.

PROFESSOR STEIN: I wonder if you would elaborate a little on the assumption of rational income- or wealth-maximizing behavior as a determinant of what happens here. You and I know that even our own government doesn't do everything that you or I might consider rational. I don't know why we should expect more rationality from the Arabs. We have great difficulty persuading the people in the United States that a high oil price is good for us. The Arab governments may have a great difficulty persuading their populations that a low oil price is good for them.

PROFESSOR HOUTHAKKER: That is true. Certainly we do not want to push the assumption of rationality too far. It happens to be the stock-in-trade of economists, and we rely on it more than we should. But let us look for a moment at what it means to be rational in this particular case. To enforce a higher price—for which I am sure there are advocates—would mean a greater reduction in output than has already taken place. That is going to be difficult. It is going to put great strains on the cohesion of OPEC. Some OPEC countries have made it clear that they want to have a fairly sizable revenue. Others seem to be more flexible about this. There are clear differences in intent and objective among the OPEC countries.

New oil discoveries will also make a difference. For instance, Venezuela has recently made important discoveries in light crude, whereas until now they had had only heavy crude. Are these light crudes going to remain in the ground forever as part of a prorationing process? It seems to me to be rather unlikely.

Perhaps Venezuela will cut back production of heavy crude sufficiently to create some room for these light crudes, but that will not be easy, because there are vested interests in maintaining a certain level of heavy crude production. Therefore, I would say that the pressures in the market are all going to be toward greater production, and considerable political effort will be necessary to reduce production.

This is where rationality comes in. If it is rational to cut back production at great political cost, perhaps it will be done. I am inclined to think that the revenue argument is going to play a role in this too, and that does not suggest that massive cutbacks really will accomplish a lot.

WALTER LEVY, Walter Levy and Associates: I have been listening with great interest to Professor Houthakker. I was particularly interested that he saw an agreement in the basic context. I think that the disagreement of Reza Fallah and Professor Houthakker couldn't be larger. Fundamentally, I don't think that you treat oil as a commodity subject to economic laws when you add to its price the future replacement value. It enters into the price, of course, twenty years ahead when we run out, but oil will never go down below $8.40 per barrel. I wonder whether we are not playing a semantic game when we claim that the oil market is a commodity market, subject to supply and demand. I think we are losing all perspective when we talk that way.

Second, Hendrik's table deals with certain models and proposes an optimal price to produce maximum revenue using these models—for instance, around $6.00 or $7.00 at 1972 prices. However, the relevant considerations for the producing country are not always to maximize any particular revenues. A government has many considerations different from those a private cartel would have. These may include the total level of reserves, rate of exhaustion, revenue needs, and revenue surpluses, which either cannot be managed or the investments eroded by inflation.

Hendrik's table shows that for an export tax rate of from $6.00 to $7.00 there is a decline in crude oil exports from the Middle East and Africa of about 3 million barrels a day or 1 billion barrels a year. This means that if these countries do not produce these 1 billion barrels they could sell it over time at at least $6.00 or $7.00 per barrel. By not producing it and reducing their revenue by $1 billion, they keep 1 billion barrels in reserve, which, using these figures, is good for a tax revenue of at least $6 or $7 billion.

In addition, when the cost of production per barrel, including depreciation, varies between twelve cents in the Middle East to eighty cents in Bolivia, how can one state that the price has to stay at $8.00 a barrel for the good of every producing country?

Do we deal with anything like a free commodity market? Do inventories really matter? Let me add one other consideration: to maximize export tax revenue at $6.00 or $7.00, there would have to be, in any case, a very substantial cut in Middle East and African production, not only below present levels of production, but even more so between present potential levels of production for 1980—assuming that nothing further is added to productive capacity during that period. There is the most extraordinary prorationing scheme built into the $6.00 or $7.00 export tax model already, because it postulates net exports at $6.00 at 18 million barrels a day. The potential right now is substantially higher and might be higher still by 1980. They have to proration under that scheme, given the potential!

If they do not proration and every country competes individually, they could return to a $1.00 export tax. This would probably be a true commodity price determined by supply availability. It would still be substantially above the cost of production from any country, including Libya, in the Middle East/African area. They would produce, then, annual exports of 47 million barrels a day instead of 17 million barrels a day, have $17 billion in revenue, and exhaust their reserves much more quickly.

I have the feeling we are living in a never-never land: The economist sets up a model. The oil-producing countries make a certain statement. We achieve an apparent agreement based on the assumption that we talk the same language. However, the language could not be more different. The goal is *not* immediate optimization of tax revenue for one particular year. That would be the aim only of a producing country that favored buying the present at the expense of the future. There is a real clash of interest—a genuine one in which each nation has good reasons to adhere to a certain policy, as it sees it in the context of its own particular economic and political condition.

Let us not hide the conflict of interests in economic jargon describing it as a commodity pattern in which the laws of economics apply and inventory accumulation determines price. If inventory accumulation will not bring the price down below $8.30, as Reza Fallah states, even though the cost of production is 20 cents, is that a free market? Can that be termed a commodity market?

CHARLES H. MURPHY, Murphy Oil Corporation: Let us concede that oil is not a renewable resource. Let us concede that governments are apt to and will view their trade in world commerce quite differently from the way in which a private corporation does. Let us concede that the language, the terminology, the jargon, if you will, is quite different from that used elsewhere. But if oil is not a commodity, what is it?

MR. LEVY: Of course it is a commodity, but is it subject to the laws of commodity trade as we know it in the London market? Is this a commodity as we have it in commodity trade in general?

PROFESSOR STEIN: Let's give Henk a chance to answer, for this is a central question.

PROFESSOR HOUTHAKKER: In the first place, this particular kind of table is calculated on what is essentially an annual basis. What Walter Levy has said and what, in a way, Dr. Fallah has said too, is that we have to take into account the replacement cost of the oil, but I have taken it into account. I have come to the conclusion that the replacement cost of the oil twenty or thirty years from now, is not going to be very much higher than it is now, because there will be practical energy alternatives at that time. Therefore, I believe it is legitimate to analyze this on an annual basis.

If we were dealing with a commodity having a supply so limited that its price would inevitably increase, or at least that it would increase faster than the real rate of interest in the economy as a whole would increase, an annual approach would not be right. In such a case, we would have to maximize not one year's revenue but a whole stream of revenues from the present to infinity. That is not necessary in the case of petroleum, because as far as I can tell—I am influenced in this by the calculations of Nordhaus and others—the price of oil is not going to rise as rapidly as the rate of interest, despite the fact that it is certainly possible that in individual countries oil supplies may run out. In the United States we have run down our supplies considerably, but other countries are still very far from doing so.

19

The disagreement, if there is one, between Walter Levy and myself, and also between Dr. Fallah and myself, is on this question: Is the price of oil going to rise by at least the rate of interest in the future or is it going to remain relatively low? That is something about which there can be disagreement, and I acknowledge the superior expertise of Dr. Fallah and Mr. Levy on this topic. But the conclusion that I have come to is that there is not going to be a significant rise in oil prices over the long run.

Now, the next question, which is also a very important one, is whether we can apply supply and demand analysis to this, in view of the fact that Dr. Fallah has said his country wants an equity price of around $8.30 per barrel. If the price is not going to be reduced, what guarantee is there that the oil will be sold? After all, there may be a surplus in the market at some point.

I've given reasons why I think a surplus may arise. I'm not saying that I'm sure about this, but I think it's a real possibility. In that case, what will Iran do? What will the other countries in the Persian Gulf do? They will presumably have to cut back production to maintain price, but that may not be in their best interest either, because the sales at that price may be very low.

What I'm saying is that the statement that the price will be kept at this low level doesn't necessarily mean this will be the policy when it comes to the crunch. It may be that not enough can be sold at the stipulated price.

One other misunderstanding might be read into Walter Levy's remarks: Is there anything uncompetitive about the fact that in the Middle East it costs twenty cents to produce oil and in the United States, it costs $5.00?

If the Middle Eastern supply is, for one reason or another, insufficient to satisfy the world demand, the price of Middle Eastern oil will be far above production cost in any case. That is just as true in a competitive market as it is in a cartelized market. The Middle East will earn a rent equal to the difference between its production cost and the cost of the highest-cost supplier whose output is demanded, which will probably be the United States.

MR. LEVY: But that is not built into this analysis, which deals with maximizing revenue. It does not take into account that this production pattern involves very substantial artificial cut-backs of supply in the Middle East. The Middle East could to a considerable extent eliminate—if it were free to produce—a large amount of the high-cost production as well.

PROFESSOR HOUTHAKKER: The reason for the tax revenue is that the rent that Middle Eastern oil obtains must be compared to the high-cost oil from the United States. That is the only reason why OPEC can levy a tax. If oil costs the same all over the world, nobody would buy OPEC oil at a higher price.

MR. LEVY: But why did they reduce production by allocation and cartel arrangements?

PROFESSOR STEIN: I think Henk's argument assumes that the cartel is trying to find out what a rational policy for the cartel is.

JOHN NASSIKAS, Federal Power Commission: My question is very simple, Professor Houthakker. You talk of a ninety-day inventory. I would like to know precisely what kind of an inventory you're talking about. Are you talking products, crude, or what? And, what is the cost of that inventory in terms of reasonably and rationally predictable prices? Finally, once we quantify the costs, would it not be a far more appropriate U.S. policy to take those economic costs and utilize these to develop our domestic resources? I find it very difficult to comprehend that we are now talking of $8.00 oil or $12.00 oil, which is close to where it is in the market today, when in the Cabinet Task Force on Oil Import Controls on which I serve, the majority of the members were talking about $1.85 oil. They assumed it could get up as high as $2.50, but it was believed this would probably not happen. And they projected that there would be $5 billion in savings to the U.S. consumer as a result of our abandonment of the quota system. I reread the task force report in brief the other day, and I was appalled at its conclusions.

PROFESSOR HOUTHAKKER: In the first place, I am not sure we want to fight the battle of the oil-import task force all over again. As we all know, there was a great deal that was wrong and, as I have said, one reason I went into energy economics was my dissatisfaction with the state of knowledge that underlay all of this. In 1969, when we worked on this task force report, the industry was telling us unanimously that the major threat was that the United States would be flooded by cheap foreign oil.

That was the one thing the industry was worried about. Maybe we should not have listened as much to industry as we did, but unfortunately that was the message we got, and it was the issue to which the report was addressed to a large extent. Apart from that, I quite agree with you that many of the things said in the report do not make good reading now.

Now considering the question of storage, let me make it clear that I wasn't actually advocating any particular storage policy. I was only saying that the fact that many countries are now accumulating inventories does have an effect on the market, and this effect will show up when they discontinue such policies.

I do not believe that a 90-day inventory is beyond our ability. I would be very dubious about a 180-day inventory, which has also been talked about. Ninety days doesn't strike me as being an unduly ambitious objective, even though I recognize that some of the money could be put into other things.

But nevertheless, inventories, if they are in the right place—I think some of them would be in the form of crude, some in the form of products—do add a great deal to our national security. That is as much as I am going to say, because I do not want to be in the position of defending any particular inventory policy.

PROFESSOR STEIN: I have a question from beyond the table: Will there be any Arab equivalent of a depletion allowance reflected in price?

PROFESSOR HOUTHAKKER: That is a somewhat complicated question. The depletion allowance is essentially a tax benefit. It does not, as such, show up in the price.

If the implication of this question is that the depletion allowance by itself increases the price, then I would say that is certainly not so. The depletion allowance may, in fact, *decrease* the price, because it makes investment in petroleum activities more profitable than it otherwise would be. But without claiming to understand the question, I would say that the depletion allowance is not relevant to this problem. It is only relevant to the taxes paid.

ELVIS J. STAHR, National Audubon Society: I, of course, am aware that this is a conference on world oil problems, but I think we need a little more perspective. One of oil's greatest uses is as a source of energy and, therefore, it needs to be looked at in the light of the total energy situation. Oil is not the only major future source of energy, and since it is nonrenewable, we are fortunate it is not the only major future source.

The world energy problem is a little different from the U.S. energy problem, I suspect. Dr. Houthakker talked rather fast past the point that nuclear energy has great possibilities. I happen to question whether it does, even in this country. I seriously wonder whether it can be proliferated around the world as, for example, an energy source for the developing countries with anything like the sort of safety which its record seems to show thus far. I do not know how many developing countries have the ability to put together controlling agencies with the kind of expertise possessed by our Atomic Energy Commission.

Furthermore, the problem is not just one of safety in the ordinary sense. Nobody has been seriously claiming that a nuclear power plant is likely to blow up like an atomic bomb. The safety problems are somewhat different, having to do with disposal of wastes, for example, and the transport and processing of materials. Most serious of all energy problems is the question of what you can do about all of the plutonium on the planet if you develop as much as you would develop if you made nuclear energy a major source of future energy.

I suspect, and there are a lot of other people who suspect, that we are going to have to turn away from reliance on nuclear power. Fortunately, the developing countries have an extraordinary amount of solar energy available to them. By

1980, it is quite practicable to contemplate a major utilization of solar energy, and it does not carry with it the dangers, or the need for regulatory commissions, that nuclear energy would obviously require. The world is going to have to turn to solar energy, since nothing else has the same potential. The sooner we set seriously about developing, the better off we will be in the long run.

At last weekend's economic summit there was one issue on which there was a clear consensus: we are going to have to make serious, substantial reductions in the consumption of energy in this country, and do this immediately. My point here is that I think this conference ought to take into account the likelihood of a major cut in energy consumption in this country. Such a cut would have many beneficial effects: helping with inflation, helping with pollution, helping with demands for capital, and helping with the balance of trade. I really think there is going to be a serious effort along these lines. I know there ought to be, and I am beginning, for the first time, to be optimistic that there very well may be.

GEORGE PIERCY, Exxon Corporation: I am impressed by the demand elasticities—something like .75—that were used in Professor Houthakker's paper. I think that this is one of the highest numbers Professor Houthakker has used lately. What do you think are the chances of your calculations being in the ball park; what is the possible error in this thing? It seems amazing to me that with $3.78 oil in the United States, we would only have 17.5 million barrels a day consumption by 1980, which is about the same, or a little less, than we have today.

PROFESSOR HOUTHAKKER: I don't really disagree with anything that Mr. Stahr has said. I am not a nuclear power enthusiast, and if solar power can be made to work reasonably well, I am not against it.

What I was saying, essentially, is that the reason the price of oil, in my opinion, is not going to rise very much over the long run, is that alternative sources of energy will be found. I mentioned nuclear power as one of these. I could also have mentioned solar energy, although that is still quite a bit further in the future. I would say that oil shale and tar sands are perhaps more important, and coal is very important, too.

Mr. Stahr feels that energy use should be cut back more. Now, actually, this in a way gets to the question raised by Mr. Piercy—namely, the elasticity figures I used. If these are too high, then we would need a tax to bring demand down to the levels shown by this table. However, I do want to assure Mr. Stahr that the demand levels used in this table are really quite low, and this is due to the price elasticity. Whether they should be even lower is something that is not clear. If I had produced another table, which was my intention, it would have shown the effects of much lower elasticities. It is true that these elasticities are a little on the high side. When I have a chance to revise this paper, I will also put in another table using much lower elasticities.

MR. PIERCY: One important factor, of course, is the time that is required for any demand elasticity to show. Now, you show a possibility of U.S. consumption going down from 18 million to 10 million barrels a day. If these demand elasticities are right, how much time do you think it will take to do that? Two decades? Three?

PROFESSOR HOUTHAKKER: I do not really think it will take that long. According to the calculations with which I am familiar, the time-lags are not all that long in the case of petroleum. But even in the case of electric power, where they are longer, they run seven years. You get 90 percent of the effect in seven years in electric power. So that is not very different from 1980.

MR. PIERCY: It is hard to see how we could cut our petroleum consumption in half by 1980 by prorationing or by any other means.

PROFESSOR HOUTHAKKER: By very high prices.

In any case, there is one argument that makes these figures come out better. The real growth rate assumed here is beginning to look very optimistic. When these calculations were first made, a 4 percent real annual growth rate for the U.S. economy from 1972 to 1980 seemed a good guess. It does not look quite as good right now. A lower growth rate would cut down the consumption on the other side.

JOHN LICHTBLAU, Petroleum Industry Research Foundation, Inc.: I have three basic comments on Mr. Piercy's observations on the elasticity assumptions in Dr. Houthakker's calculations. I have no problem with the table as such and with the concept.

Obviously Dr. Houthakker assumes that OPEC is a well-functioning cartel. As such, it controls the price. The cartel seeks an optimum price for the commodity which is controlled, which needn't be, and usually isn't, the maximum price, but it is a price that maximizes revenue. Such a price does exist in theory, and it also exists somewhat in practice. The OPEC nations may ignore their optimum price and may suboptimize their revenues. Nevertheless, an optimum price does exist somewhere, and it can be calculated.

What bothers me here is the specific optimum price of $6.00. If it were anything like that, our problems would be a lot less severe than they appear to be. The number makes a tremendous difference, because we are currently producing something like 23-24 million barrels of oil from the Middle East and Africa. At a price of $10.00 per barrel, which isn't that much higher than what we have now, Dr. Houthakker concludes that production of exports will go down to 7 million barrels a day between now and 1980, and that this will be offset to a small extent by a 3-million-barrel-a-day increase in U.S. production. This would mean a radical decline in world oil consumption within six years, which could only result from a major recession or depression.

If, on the other hand, that $6.00 price is much too low, and the optimum price is really $9.00 or $10.00, then we will get the oil we need, but it would mean almost unbearable monetary terms. Either way, we have a major problem. As Dr. Houthakker said correctly, in the short run, energy conservation is determined by the stock of energy-using equipment, and that stock is not going to change significantly between now and 1980.

I think a different optimum price, perhaps a more realistic one, would show that we have some very serious problems here. While this one shows that things are going to improve, I do not think they will improve.

PROFESSOR HOUTHAKKER: I have the impression you were saying this can't be right because everybody knows how bad things are and this note of cheerfulness is out of place. I would say that the $10.00 price line is pretty extreme. What it means is not really a tremendous reduction in energy use, but a massive shift to coal. That is really what it amounts to. There is an awful lot of coal around the world, and most of it is not being very well used.

India, for instance, has large coal reserves. These could be brought into production. I do not know how likely it is, but it certainly is a possibility. And there are many other parts of the world where coal occurs in sizable quantities. There is implicit in this table a shift within the energy sector.

I also do not agree with Mr. Lichtblau's remark that the stock of energy-using equipment will be the same in 1980 as it is now. I think by 1980 there will already be a massive readjustment in the energy-using stock, and this need not take long.

The lifetime of cars in the United States is something like seven or eight years. The cars that are on the road now will practically all be gone by 1980. And the newer cars that will take their place will almost certainly consume less gasoline.

MR. LICHTBLAU: Or more.

PROFESSOR HOUTHAKKER: It could be, but that is not very likely, I think.

MR. LICHTBLAU: It depends on air-pollution requirements and that sort of thing. It is not clear that the 1976 models will not be less efficient than the '75 models.

MR. ROYSTER: This is peripheral to the world oil situation, but I would just like your opinion on the rationale for the proposed gasoline tax in this country.

PROFESSOR HOUTHAKKER: I do not particularly like the idea of singling out gasoline for a tax. It would really make more sense to have a tax on a broad range of energy resources, including even natural gas and electric power.

MR. ROYSTER: Well, if tying a tax to it would, in effect, help the situation, there is a presumption of high elasticity in the demand for it. But are you not also saying that the Middle East people are not really charging enough if we can get the same effect by having the whole world oil price go up even higher?

PROFESSOR STEIN: Sure we could, but we do not want to pay it to them. We would rather pay it to the U.S. Treasury. That's a tremendous difference. Maybe this is the third-best solution, but we are probably operating now with the fifth or sixth best.

MR. ROYSTER: Your rationale makes more sense than any economic argument I've heard before.

PROFESSOR STEIN: I think I am making an economic argument: it pays better to have the money yourself than to give it to somebody else.

MELVIN R. LAIRD, *Reader's Digest* and the AEI National Energy Project: There is the political argument, too, which has to be considered when you look into the use of the gasoline tax, because the gasoline tax can be used in other ways. The tax is not only a means of bringing the revenue into the U.S. government rather than sending it abroad. It also can be used to produce some public awareness of the problem of conservation.

Gasoline consumption is going up in this country, not down. The gasoline tax would be a means of encouraging car-pooling and other kinds of conservation activities. Combined with a rationing system, the effect could be quite significant.

People who have to drive to and from work should not pay any kind of increase in gasoline. Such people should get their refunds, complete and total refunds. People that use car-pools should get double refunds.

In any case, I think sooner or later a tough gasoline-rationing system is going to be needed in the United States, because there is no public awareness of the energy problem we face. Right now $100 billion is moving from the developed world to another section of the world, and the total will be $600 billion over the next six years. That is equal to more than the total value of everything on the New York stock exchange with a Dow Jones average of about 750. It's equal to three times the total monetary reserves of all the free nations of the world, and it calls for conservation. We are not facing up to the need for conservation as far as this country is concerned.

MR. NASSIKAS: I am in full accord with Mr. Laird's views on conservation. We preach this all over the country and will continue to do so. However, we have to evaluate the extent to which conservation will help to resolve the full problem, and we must conclude that it will not.

26

Currently we use 25 percent of our primary energy resources for electricity. By almost any forecast, with very limited growth, compounded at 3 percent or even 2 percent, we will still be utilizing about 50 percent of our energy resources for production of electricity by the year 2000.

With regard to nuclear power: the largest single measure we can take to conserve our fossil fuel resources in this country, to maintain our energy objectives and our energy independence, would be to develop a nuclear capacity capable of generating about 50 percent of all electric power within the next twenty years. The balance should be generated by coal-fired plants.

With such a program, we could release the equivalent of more than all the fossil fuel resources used to generate electric power in the year 1974. That is what I would like to suggest as a conservation program, emphasizing that I am as concerned with safety and with human welfare as is the next person.

DR. FALLAH: Much of your earlier discussion was devoted to suggestions of cut-backs and prorationing in order to keep prices high. As far as Iran is concerned, we have never agreed to cut-backs. In fact, our sovereign is on public record as having opposed them and having recommended the withdrawal of the Arab cutbacks.

Our policy is to equate supply with demand, never to produce a shortage whereby people suffer or industries have to close down. But, at the same time, we will not produce a surplus which nobody wants whereby prices would come down.

PROFESSOR STEIN: I guess the question is whether you are going to equate supply and demand at $10.00 or $1.00. [Laughter.]

PART TWO

Canadian Energy Problems:
A Microcosm of the World Situation

During the luncheon session, Minister Donald S. Macdonald used the example of resource depletion, resource pricing, terms of trade, and income distribution between Canada's western energy-producing provinces and eastern energy-consuming provinces to delineate the world oil situation.

CANADIAN ENERGY PROBLEMS: A MICROCOSM OF THE WORLD SITUATION

WILLIAM J. BAROODY, American Enterprise Institute: In this country when people think of oil imports they tend to think of the Middle East. Yet the United States, as I understand it, actually imports far more oil from Canada than from any Middle Eastern nation.

Thus, Canadian energy policy is of critical importance to the United States. U.S. oil import policy toward Canada and Canadian oil export policy toward the United States have changed considerably in recent years. A few years ago the U.S. was restricting imports from Canada. Now we pay a sizable tax and take all the oil we can get.

We are fortunate indeed to have with us today the Canadian minister of energy, mines and resources, the Honorable Donald S. Macdonald. [Applause.]

DONALD S. MACDONALD, Government of Canada: It is always a pleasure for a Canadian to come south, particularly at this time of year—a pleasure modified, however, in my case, by the fact that I will miss the telecast of the sixth game of the Canada-Soviet Union hockey series. If anyone hears the score during my talk, and it is good news, I would be grateful if he would shout it out. [Laughter.]

Last week I had the opportunity of taking part in the World Energy Conference in Detroit. It struck me at that time that one of the benefits of the massive disturbance in the world energy situation over the past year is that now, finally, we are looking at our problems together—technical experts, pure scientists, resource producers, industrial consumers, even mere politicians. I carefully choose my words in saying that we are "finally" getting together. The problem of insatiable demand in the face of peaking production in some major producing areas, with the inescapable consequence of soaring prices, has been visible, though on a seemingly distant horizon, for the better part of this decade. What has happened is that the events of the past winter have rocketed us forward to that horizon, and while it has been a turbulent journey, an unsettling twelve months that threatened to disrupt the established patterns of international trade, we are at the point where an analysis of the world energy situation is finally being made at the senior level.

Faced with the consequent peril to our economic order and well-being, we are in danger, perhaps, of becoming disoriented and of blaming all the problems in the world on the leaping prices of energy resources. I consider it essential to grasp that indeed the days of cheap energy are well and truly over, but the actions of OPEC only moved that day of reckoning closer. It was an inevitable horizon that was going to catch up to us in any event. Had the actions of OPEC last fall and this year taken place in a world where all countries—not just the rich, but all countries—were enjoying healthy economic growth, where inflation was under control, where doomsday predictions about an ever-increasing demand against limited resources had not become a cult, then I think it would have been easier to understand our predicament. It would have been easier for us to pan out a few nuggets of truth. In fact, it would have been possible for the world to come in a measured way to the clear recognition that the long-run costs of resource supplies were steadily rising and the inevitable result would be a severe problem both in the redistribution of economic rents accruing to the lower-cost producers and in the redistribution of real income between the producing areas and the consuming areas, between the "have" and the "have-not" nations. If we had had that longer time frame, the world would have had time to quantify the long-run costs of new resource exploitation and ensure rational development.

Unfortunately, we were unable to follow this happy script of an easier adjustment to higher resource costs. It is true that the world has enjoyed over two decades of unparalleled growth, but this growth has had a number of disquieting features. In the first place, disappointment has awaited those who trusted that, with the rapid growth in the industrial world, we would have better living standards in the developing world, that this growth would narrow the disparities between rich and poor.

Apart from a fortunate few, growth in the underdeveloped world has been agonizingly slow. By the late 1960s, we had become infected with an inflation that seemed to have acquired an immunity to traditional cures. By the early 1970s, most of the Western world was for the first time encountering a double-digit inflation aggravated by intractable material and food shortages. These shortages and the sustained growth rates of demand which led to them—most notably, the growing shortage of natural gas in the United States and the increasing dependency of the United States and other industrial nations on imported crude oil—began to focus concern on the long-range adequacy of supplies. And at the same time, an anxiety was also aroused about the capacity of the world to feed its expanding population. To all of this was added the awakening concern about our environment, especially the threat of damage to the biosphere from the development and consumption of extractive resources and, particularly, fossil fuels.

The result has been no little confusion, and I fear we all suffer from it. I would like to try to put some of this confusion to rest. My aim is to disentangle the components of the problem and to provide some direction for its possible solution. In order to achieve that, I would propose to take the parochial course of describing my own country's situation, because I feel that in many respects the problems in Canada on the energy scene are a microcosm of the world situation.

As you know, Canada is a federal state composed of a group of provinces. The individual provinces have the ultimate ownership of natural resources, and these resources are unevenly distributed. Some provinces have an abundance. Others have few, if any, mineral and energy resources. Some regions of Canada have higher levels of real income, and growth rates in others, compared to the country as a whole, have been uneven.

In short, Canada has a severe regional imbalance problem. During the 1950s and the 1960s, the terms of trade in Canada moved against the resource-producing provinces, and only in this decade has there been a reversal, with the terms of trade beginning to move sharply in favor of the energy-rich provinces. On the basis of prices that were declining through the last two decades, Canadian consumption of both oil and natural gas grew rapidly. However, the realization is full upon us that Canada's conventional supplies of crude oil and natural gas from currently accessible reservoirs are limited and that they are being rapidly exhausted. The National Energy Board found for the first time in 1970 that there was insufficient natural gas, surplus to foreseeable Canadian needs, to permit new exports sought by U.S. customers.

Since then, only minor quantities of gas have been approved for export, although some 42 percent of our gas production is currently going to export markets through previous authorization. It now appears that Canadian oil and gas production from our conventional resources in currently accessible reservoirs is peaking out, and peaking out only a short time after the peaking of production in the United States.

We have in our country the potential for alternative supplies from the frontiers, but this potential is available only at sharply higher cost levels. Exploration is now taking place in the Arctic and off our east coast, with some encouraging results, particularly with respect to natural gas. The Athabasca oil sands, whose existence has been known for generations, are now beginning to be developed. However, on the basis of present information, it may be the late 1980s before significant volumes of oil will be available from all these new potential sources. Massive capital investment will be required in exploration, production, and transportation facilities to bring this new oil and gas to market, and certainly, the market price will have to be significantly higher than the prices that have prevailed in the past.

Another feature that makes the Canadian situation a microcosm of the world is our geography. Because of the breadth of the country and the concentration of petroleum resources in western Canada, one half of the country has been wholly dependent on imported oil supplies, while the other has been largely an exporter to the United States. Early in the 1970s, exports of crude oil began to burgeon. By 1973, crude oil shipments to the United States were almost double the level of

1970—that is to say, they were just over a million barrels a day. At the same time, imports into our eastern provinces were steadily rising.

A final aspect of Canada's situation that is relevant to the world scene is that we too are in the grip of inflation. While it is slightly less severe than that suffered by some other industrialized countries, it is occurring nonetheless at a double-digit rate. When OPEC prices advanced rapidly through the fall of last year, the eastern half of Canada was threatened with a sharp decline in the terms of trade and a substantial loss in real income. On the other hand, if prices had been allowed to follow world levels, the oil-producing provinces would have stood to gain enormously by the transfer in real income from consumers. Given the background of inflation and the magnitude of the potential income transfer, there is understandably a very substantial resistance to permitting the resource-producing provinces to follow world levels in setting prices for domestic resources.

The essential principle upon which Canadian policy was formed involved the attempt both to be clear on the real costs of future Canadian supplies and to use, accept, the real costs as a target for domestic pricing policies. In moving to this price level—that is, to the real cost price level—over a period of two or three years, or perhaps longer, some concession had to be made to consuming interests and to the concern over inflation.

The rents created by the advance of the price for conventional reserves were employed in part to limit the exposure of the importing half of the country to international prices. In this situation, the federal government attempted to play the the role of arbiter of an efficient pricing policy and then to use its influence to secure an equitable redistribution of some of the remaining rent in order to ameliorate the painful consequences of the price increase itself by transfers to the consuming regions. This objective was not an easy one to reach, and it did not go uncriticized. Indeed, some of the criticism emanated not very far from the spot on which I now stand. So I think it is appropriate, in addition to giving you the philosophy behind our goals, to underline briefly a few basic considerations.

The price of Canadian oil to U.S. consumers did not go up because of the export tax. Rather, the Canadian price followed international price levels—the prices that we have to pay for oil in eastern Canada. The export tax was a purely domestic matter. It was the means of determining among different Canadian interests, consuming and producing, who would get the benefit of the increased economic rent. To fulfill our aim of easing the burden on our eastern consumers of higher offshore prices, we instead used these new returns from export sales as a cushion. We believed then, and we still believe today, that this is a purely domestic matter. We hold to the same belief in regard to natural gas prices. Our policy is to bring the price of natural gas into line with the market values of competitive fuels, both from the standpoint of conserving a valuable, nonrenewable resource and for the stimulation of development. We will do so in a staged fashion in order to cushion the impact on both U.S. and Canadian consumers. As you know, the border price of 1,000 cubic feet of gas will be set at $1.00 on 1 January 1975, and the near future also holds increases for domestic gas prices—although not necessarily to the levels of export prices, since the market values of competing fuel oils in Canada have been held below international prices by federal-provincial agreement. As I have said, we believe that this, too, is an internal matter among Canadians.

My purpose in reviewing the Canadian experience is, as I indicated, to attempt to create a model for a view of world problems. But before coming to the forbidding problems of international distribution, and of the reallocation of real income, let me first try to tackle the question of world pricing of energy resources, that is, the question of the purely efficient solution, leaving aside for the moment the distribution issues.

There have been worthy studies that have struggled with the problem of providing meaningful estimates of world fossil fuel resources and of alternate energy sources. While I sense an emerging consensus on the availability of fossil fuels, the literature on alternate energy sources varies widely from the technologically optimistic to the technologically pessimistic. On the demand side, the literature embraces the remarkably sanguine view of Dale Jorgenson and Edward Hudson at Harvard, and of the Ford Foundation's Energy Policy Project—the view that a substantial portion of the substitution over the past three decades in favor of capital and energy and against labor is reversible if energy prices rise sufficiently.

According to this view, the United States could achieve virtually zero energy growth by the year 2000, with less than a 5 percent reduction in the gross national product that would have been achieved by that year were energy consumption to continue to grow at recent rates. On the other hand, the elasticity pessimists cite both the lack of relevant historical experience and the association of energy consumption with real standards of living to conclude that price will bring little relief in demand.

Economists have, however, come to understand again that even a low negative price elasticity, when accumulated over twenty-five years, will have substantial consequences. To return then to the supply side, there would appear to be some consensus that if present consumption rates continue, fossil fuels—or at least oil and gas—will be exhausted sometime in the middle of the twenty-first century. Available uranium supplies at less than $15.00 a pound would extend this estimate by twenty-five years with current nuclear reactors and by seventy-five years with breeder reactors. If uranium rose to $30.00 a pound, one might add an additional 100 years with the breeder reactor.

The increase that may occur in these estimates as a result of technological breakthroughs in the areas of fusion, hydrogen, and solar conversion, to name only three, is of course, immense. Nonetheless, based on current knowledge, it is difficult to avoid the conclusion that OPEC performed a service, albeit a painful one, by focusing attention on rapidly depleting world supplies of fossil fuel. This conclusion is strengthened by the recognition that the world may have better alternate uses for its hydrocarbons in the manufacture of fertilizer than as a source of protein.

Frankly, I am unable to conclude what the world price should now be, but I think that the struggle to find that efficiency price is a critical one. Or rather, I think, the formation of a consensus around what will always be a fuzzy concept is of critical importance. I have only to remind you of another portion of the literature which plays "catch 22" games regarding the possible breakup of OPEC and the possible overinvestment by the rest of the world, at too high a cost, in alternatives. The world is aware, of course, that underpricing these resources can result in a crisis of scarcity. Clearly, a more precise view of the real price of these resources must be found. Further, until technological alternatives become more clearly recognized, the restraint of demand, particularly in the industrial world that now consumes 75 percent of the total annual energy production, not only is in order, but also should have high priority.

I must now deal with the problems arising from the uneven distribution of world resources, the problems of a redistribution of true rents, and particularly the problems facing the world as a result of OPEC action. Let me say first that I believe OPEC prices are currently above the point on the curve of the world's long-run resource costs. So it is inaccurate to characterize all of current OPEC returns as rents. To a large degree, it is our belief, they are monopoly profits. I make that point for two reasons: first, because we in Canada, as consumers of imported oil, are as unhappy as anybody else about the dramatic nature of the price increase and would be as happy as anyone else to see a reduction in the costs of imported oil. Secondly, in the context of future world energy policy, we believe we must disentangle the general problem of rent, which will continuously recur over all extractive resources. I do not believe that the way out of this problem is by a subscription to either cost-of-service or vintage pricing. In fact, vintage pricing has been, in my view, a principal element in present world problems. It leads to inefficient and excessive use of resources and breeds justified hostility on the part of the resource owner.

Extractive, nonrenewable resources play a preponderant role in the exports of the less-developed countries. To deny these rents is to deny a just return from commodities that have historically been and will continue to be enormously variable in price. Having said this, I would quickly acknowledge that occasionally these economic rents will far exceed the capacity of the receiving country to spend and painfully strain the capacity of the consuming countries to pay. These higher rents may exacerbate world inflation. Our task, then, is to learn to distinguish justified changes in real, relative prices from purely inflationary movement. We will have to rely on an expanded ability of the world capital market to extend the periods of adjustment to transfer real income.

36

This then leads me to some final comments on the larger issue of real income distribution in the world. Whatever conservation can be achieved in the industrialized countries through higher prices and the more prudent use of resources, it is obvious that mechanisms must be found to ensure that the product of this massive investment is equitably shared on a worldwide basis. The relationship, at least up to a point, between energy and real standards of living is too strong to be denied. To achieve this more equitable distribution of at least minimal sources of energy, as with food and other essential commodities, is the single challenge that dominates all others.

EDWARD COWAN, the *New York Times:* Would you clarify the sentence in which you said that it might be the late 1980s before significant volumes of oil will be available from all these new potential sources. For "all" would you substitute "any"?

MR. MACDONALD: If you are talking about the Canadian frontier, I think that "significant volume" is obviously a qualification as well. It will be difficult to have a significant contribution, say, from the Mackenzie Delta or the Beaufort Sea, where we have identified the oil potential, or from the Atlantic offshore, where we have not identified any very substantial oil reserves. It will be difficult for this oil to be received in Canadian markets or American markets before that time frame.

The principal problem is further exploration, which involves the difficulty of exploring offshore in water which is not only deep but also ice-infested. In addition, there are all the problems of putting in a pipeline link.

If you are probing at my expectation with regard to the Athabasca oil sands development, I would have to say that while one can expect there to be a certain rhythm in the expansion of oil sands production, this will not be dramatic. The most dramatic change that will occur in this regard, if it is to occur, will have to be the development of more economical means of getting at the larger part of this deposit, which is *in situ* beyond the current technology.

MR. COWAN: What about natural gas in the Mackenzie Delta?

MR. MACDONALD: That potential could be on a shorter time frame. As you know, there are at the moment a number of applications outstanding before the Federal Power Commission, and one is outstanding in Canada, dealing with bringing North Slope or Arctic Ocean resources—natural gas resources—to the southern markets. I would hesitate to comment on how quickly the regulatory stage would be dealt with, but it could be that Canadian gas might come into the Canadian and possibly American markets in the late 1970s. As to when Alaskan gas will be coming into the lower forty-eight states, I will not make any predictions.

JIM BISHOP, *Newsweek* magazine: I would like to pick up on your comment about the OPEC price being above the curve. How effective do you think the recent statements by President Ford and Secretary of State Kissinger have been in getting that price into a better position on the curve? Do you think they were basically productive, or counterproductive?

MR. MACDONALD: I think that is a little difficult to judge in the short run. If their statements are to be judged by whether or not OPEC prices come down in this subsequent week, then I think they would have to be regarded as not having been productive. But I assume that the U.S. administration is following a very carefully concerted plan in setting forth on this particular line of discussion, and I think we will have to await future events to see whether, indeed, the prices do come down. Spokesmen both in the United States and, indeed, among the OPEC nations have indicated the possibility of a drop in the world price by as much as $2.00. I think we will have to wait to see the cumulative results of this kind of essentially political campaign.

STANLEY BENJAMIN, Associated Press: You said that you assume that such statements are part of a concerted plan, and I cannot help noticing that you made a point of inserting a statement into your prepared remarks to the effect that Canada would like to see the price come down. Is your statement, perhaps, part of the same plan?

MR. MACDONALD: Frankly my reason for making the point, for inserting it into the text, was to emphasize with this audience and with the wider American audience that we do not have a vested interest in high OPEC prices, that we have to pay them ourselves. We have to bring in 900 thousand or a million barrels a day from overseas, and we would rather use the economic rents from our oil production for other purposes here in Canada than have to pay them abroad. Therefore, we have a common interest in lower prices.

As to where OPEC oil prices should be, we would try to estimate in our own country that frontier resources, whether you are talking about conventional oil in the Beaufort Sea or oil-sands oil, are going to be more expensive than those we are now producing from in Alberta; we see an inevitable increase in the cost. However, we certainly would welcome a $2.00 decrease in Canada.

MR. BENJAMIN: Sir, could I ask you about the competing pipeline applications, which, as you note, Chairman Nassikas is going to have to wrestle with. It seems to me that Canada's attitude towards the Mackenzie Delta line would have something to do with the viability of the other line, as well as the one to Alaska. It would be a kind of toss-up. You are not going to have both.

Does the filing of the competing all-Alaska pipeline and tanker route, which would not go through Canada, influence Canada's attitude toward these controversial questions of Canadian ownership and Canadian control over the line, the sharing of the volumes going through it, and so forth? The Canadian decision would presumably influence our decision to the extent that it affects the amount of gas we get.

MR. MACDONALD: I would say first that this is, of course, not unanticipated. We have known that El Paso has been toiling away in preparation for this situation. I would say equally that we don't see, at least in general terms, any problems arising from the alternative proposal by the Canadian Arctic Task Study Group. Naturally, they will have to satisfy the appropriate tribunals in Canada with regard to environmental and other problems, but having done so, we don't feel threatened by the proposal. Indeed, this fits into a proposal which Prime Minister Trudeau has made, and to which we would give high priority now. That is, that this is a good time for Canadian and American authorities to sit down and to discuss a treaty or, if the United States would prefer, an executive agreement for the purpose of mutually securing pipeline transit across each other's countries.

When we hear people suggesting that our country would be an unsafe area of transit for an American pipeline, we are always mindful of the fact that in the dead of winter, all of the oil that is in Montreal and Toronto markets crosses U.S. territory and that a very substantial portion of our natural gas does too. We would have to be particularly maladroit if we got into a situation in which we had no American gas to assist our own markets, but found ourselves being cut off because of actions we took. In other words, we think that there is a natural affinity between our two countries, and that the Mackenzie line would very clearly carry American gas to American users. It would use the transit of Canada for this purpose, and it would make sense to get the insecurity argument out of the way by negotiating this kind of a treaty. We will give a security agreement high priority, so that the Mackenzie Delta Pipeline can be considered on its own merits.

MR. BENJAMIN: You, obviously, are a Canadian authority on this subject, and Chairman Nassikas is an American authority (I do not notice any State Department representatives here). Are you and Chairman Nassikas going to discuss that kind of agreement while you are in Washington?

MR. MACDONALD: Perhaps Chairman Nassikas had better answer that, but I think that he would probably say that there are other responsible agencies in the administration that he might think should be brought into such a discussion as well. I think that this is an important early discussion; indeed, our representatives here in Washington have been canvassing the State Department on this subject.

MR. BENJAMIN: At the beginning of this year, both Canadian and American government officials were saying that talks on the subject of the line treaty or executive agreement would be well under way by this time. What is the hang-up?

MR. MACDONALD: I think that the hang-up, principally, was political events in both countries. I will not comment on the political events in this country, but Canada has returned to a new and more rational stable situation since the July 8 election. We now feel a greater freedom of action in many areas—not the least in this one. I think it is fair to say that our attention may have been a little distracted by political events at home.

ROSS MONROE, *Toronto Globe and Mail:* Last December, Prime Minister Trudeau seemed to commit his government, in principle, to the concept of a line carrying both Alaskan and Mackenzie Delta natural gas. In the light of the announcement by Alberta Gas Trunk, has the Trudeau government changed its position on that matter, or is it moving toward a position of neutrality vis-à-vis what now appears to be shaping up as two competing proposals?

MR. MACDONALD: I would have to say that neutrality was our principal concern in December of 1973 and was reflected in the prime minister's statement. In the Canadian administrative and political process, we should consider as soon as possible the desirability of having a Mackenzie pipeline carrying Alaskan gas to the United States, and there could be an associated line for the purpose of carrying Mackenzie Valley gas. There are obvious economies to be attained for Canadian gas and gas users if our gas is traveling through a conduit that is also carrying larger volumes to the United States.

The political discussion over a period of time, concerning the oil pipeline, the one that has been superseded by TAP: We thought it was desirable to stimulate an early application, to get this question out before the regular jury tribunal and out before the Canadian people. The prime minister stipulated a condition, which I mentioned just a moment ago—namely, that this, of course, is subject to approvals of the appropriate tribunals in Canada and that condition remains.

CHARLES MURPHY, Murphy Oil Corporation: As the first export customer of Canadian crude, could we become more specific concerning transit accommodations? As you know, the National Energy Board is throttling back on the supply of oil to the upper Midwest in the United States—a matter of very great concern to those states, to their congressional delegation, and to the administraion. Would Canada's cooperation, which is expressed in general concerning transit, extend to the specific point of reversing the flow of the Edmonton to Puget Sound crude oil pipeline—

MR. MACDONALD: Transmountain? Yes.

MR. MURPHY: —and then tying into the existing inter-provincial system, so as to make Alaskan crude available early on to the heart of the United States which you are now warning us that you can no longer supply?

MR. MACDONALD: I would have to say two things: First, we do anticipate that there will be a reduction of Canadian exports to the United States. One of the factors that we would, however, be taking into account in our relationship is that there are a number of refineries in the northern tier that came into being specifically because of Canadian oil, that certainly have a dependence that we would recognize, and that would receive priority in our long-range policy on oil exports. I think that it is clear that we have *some* time in which to adjust this relationship.

On the question of whether we would accept Alyeska oil in effect in Vancouver and put it over Transmountain, there are some problems involved in doing that, in terms of the environmental problem of bringing heavy movements into Vancouver harbor. And there is the question, of course, as to our own national policy in this regard. But it is certainly a subject upon which we would be prepared to hear more, in due course. We follow that with interest, and it does seem to be the means of meeting the problems of middle-western refineries.

STUART PERRY, Environmental Action, Inc.: Are you unalterably opposed to higher prices to promote energy conservation practices?

MR. MACDONALD: Not unalterably. It depends upon the level to which you want to go. From our national policy standpoint, we have accepted the inevitability of higher prices—at least to the level at which we can provide for alternative sources in Canada. On the other hand, prices that would result in an undue shift of real income from consuming areas to producing areas—those we would oppose. But we accept the general concept of a price increase, also recognizing that there is a benefit from that in terms of conservation and therefore from an environmental standpoint.

MR. COWAN: There has been some talk about the efforts of the principal importing and industrial nations to reduce their consumption and importation of crude oil. Do you think that would be a useful way to approach the price problem? And would Canada be willing to curtail these imports to contribute to that effort?

MR. MACDONALD: I think that the principal forum in which that was discussed was a meeting last weekend to which we were not invited. Therefore, we are not really prepared to accept the conclusions of that meeting until we have fuller information. In the long run, we recognize the importance of restraining consumption in order both to preserve our domestic resources and, indeed, to lessen the impact of overseas costs. We would be prepared to cooperate in discussions in this particular respect, and we look forward to being invited to them when they occur. [Laughter.]

PART THREE

The Politics of World Oil

In his presentation, Professor George Lenczowski argued that oil is a unique commodity, one whose treatment in both producing and consuming nations is greatly influenced by political considerations. He examined the problem since 1973 as involving two major components: the crisis of production cutbacks and embargoes and the crisis of prices. He then presented a discussion of the politico-economic policies of the major oil producing and consuming nations in meeting these twin crises and the potential in this situation for confrontations replacing rational discussions and quiet diplomacy.

THE POLITICS OF WORLD OIL

WILLIAM J. BAROODY, American Enterprise Institute: I would like to start off by noting that the economists had their say this morning, and it is now time to take up the more serious subject of the politics of world oil. AEI's National Energy Project is very much concerned with research into the political aspects of the energy issue, as well as into the economic and other aspects. Future studies and programs in its series will cover the political side of both domestic and international energy questions.

To chair the session, we have quite naturally turned to a professional politician, the Honorable Philip Ruppe, U.S. representative from the eleventh district of Michigan. As is true, with so many of our leaders in this seat of government, he has been affiliated with the University of Michigan, although he did take time out at one point to obtain a degree from Yale.

Mr. Ruppe was elected to the Congress in 1966, has been returned three times, and makes a fourth try next month. He serves on the House Committee on Interior and Insular Affairs and is ranking minority member on its Environmental Subcommittee.

PHILIP E. RUPPE, U.S. House of Representatives (R-Mich.): Thank you very much. I am certainly pleased to be here and as one who will stand for reelection within thirty days, I am sure I will be one of the principal gainers from the comments and observations that will be expressed here this afternoon.

It is my pleasure to introduce our afternoon speaker. Professor Lenczowski, who has quite a record in academic circles in the United States, currently serves as professor of political science at the University of California at Berkeley. He was born in Russia—rather incidentally, perhaps, inasmuch as he is a decendant of an old Polish family and served in the Polish Foreign Service from 1938 to 1945. Among his published works are *Russia and the West in Iran, 1918-1948, The Middle East in World Affairs,* and *Oil and State in the Middle East.* He serves as a member of the American Enterprise Institute's Advisory Board, and he is also on the Board of Governors of the Middle East Institute.

GEORGE LENCZOWSKI, University of California: There is something unique about oil among the world's commodities. It is a resource which is plentiful and

45

yet exhaustible. It is largely concentrated in the Middle East, which is not only an area of traditional strategic importance and great power rivalries, but also the site of some of the most persistent international conflicts. Finally, oil is a commodity without which, and in the absence of an adequate and practical substitute, civilization of the advanced West such as we know it today would suffer a relapse of deep and dramatic proportions.

A rational approach to the utilization of this depletable resource would dictate a systematic pursuance of three objectives: (1) conservation of the existing reserves and avoidance of waste, (2) search for and development of new oil fields, and (3) research into and development of additional substitute forms of energy. The paradox is that while in our seemingly rational Western world there was no mystery about the right course of action in this respect, we had to be shaken out of complacency by two major crises which overlapped each other in 1973-74—the crisis of production cutbacks and embargoes and the crisis of prices.

Each of these crises had a different origin. The production crisis stemmed from the decision of the Arab states to use oil as a weapon in their political struggle, a struggle which was dramatized by the fourth Arab-Israeli war of October 1973. The price crisis had an economic motivation. The spectacular quadrupling of oil prices was initiated by Iran, a non-Arab country, at a meeting in Teheran in December 1973 and was adopted by other member-states of the Organization of Petroleum Exporting Countries (OPEC) for reasons that not only had nothing to do—or little to do—with the attainment of Arab boycott objectives, but actually contradicted it. Although the Arab production cutback policy was aimed at penalizing foes and rewarding friends, the drastic price hike hurt friend and foe alike, thus nullifying to a certain extent the benefits expected to be gained from the boycott strategy.

The two crises, therefore, were different in nature and in scope—one being of short duration (though with a potential of being repeated) and the other affecting the world on a long-range basis. However, they had in common the fact that both resulted not from the normal economic workings of the market mechanism but from sovereign decisions of independent governments. Moreover, although the two crises had different origins—one political and the other economic—they became conceptually interconnected in that price regulation would have been impossible to achieve without the demonstrated ability to control production.

The sovereign role of the governments in producing the two crises represents an end of an evolutionary chain which contained three distinct phases:

(1) In the first phase of the companies' supremacy, the oil companies were determining production and setting prices. They also operated on the basis of long-range concessions, owned the necessary assets, and fully controlled and managed the operations. It was a situation in which the market mechanism was functioning.

46

(2) The second phase, as I see it, was the phase of negotiation, which dates back to the establishment of OPEC in the 1960s. The host governments began to assert and secure the right to have a voice in the determination of prices, and their influence on allocation and levels of production was debated. It was still an era of the buyers' market. Hence the proposed and controversial prorating formula was to serve the production expansion of certain states while safeguarding the others against the shrinking of their output.

(3) We are now in the phase of government supremacy. In this third and last phase, the host governments have assumed the exclusive right to determine the levels of production and of prices, have staked and secured a partial claim to their right to determine the volume of supplies to individual recipients, and increasingly but unevenly have acquired the control and management of operations. The new notions and slogans of this period call for a shift from concession to service contract, from negotiation to legislation, from mere taxes and royalties to participation or full ownership. The role of the companies is being gradually reduced to technical and commercial-distributive tasks. Decisions affecting the long-range planning and financial allocations for development are increasingly devolving upon the host governments.

Given the acknowledged fact of the current supremacy of the producing governments, it is relevant to establish their identity, objectives, and methods.

As for identity, the heterogeneous composition of the producing camp is often blissfully ignored. This group includes states in the Middle East as well as those in Black Africa, Latin America, the Far East, and, as Minister Macdonald pointed out earlier, North America as well. In the Middle East and North Africa, it is composed of non-Arab Iran and a group of Arab states, the latter differing from each other politically and in terms of general development. Thus, under their respective revolutionary regimes, Iraq and Libya adopt an attitude critical of the West, while the more conservative Saudi Arabia, the Gulf states, and Kuwait maintain close relations with the Western world. Moreover, these conservative Arab states, together with revolutionary Libya, have a limited technological absorptive capacity and, with the rise of oil prices, are certain to accumulate considerable surplus cash reserves. By contrast, Iran, Iraq, and Algeria, a very mixed group ideologically and ethnically, have a much higher capacity to absorb the influx of funds and to funnel them into a rapid development process.

Concern for conservation also varies considerably from country to country. It has emerged as a significant factor in Saudi Arabia, Kuwait, Iran, and to some extent in Libya, but is overshadowed by concern for income-maximizing in Algeria and Iraq.

These differing objectives and priorities have influenced the methods employed by the producing states in furtherance of their oil policies. Saudi Arabia, because of political objectives relating to the Arab-Israeli conflict and also because of its long-range concern with conservation, has stood in the forefront of the Arab states which declared an embargo against the United States, South Africa, Holland, and Portugal in 1973. In fact, Saudi Arabia's stand on this matter was decisive for the entire Arab oil strategy activated by the October War. By contrast, Iran's main objective was to maximize revenue, which involved emphasis on price levels. Interestingly enough, the Arab state of Iraq did not follow the majority of the Arab countries in decreeing production cutbacks. Instead, it concentrated on taking over American interests in the multinational Basrah Petroleum Company. Libya, for its part, adopted a mixed policy of partial nationalization and production cutbacks. At the same time, revenue-thirsty Algeria, while following the general Arab boycott policies, impatiently awaited the lifting of restrictions so that it could resume and even increase production. I remember having lunch with the oil minister of Algeria a short time before the embargo was removed, and he complained bitterly about having to follow the general Arab policy in this respect because it did not suit Algeria's revenue objectives.

On the price issue, the general solidarity in the producing camp was more evident. Because of its nonpolitical, economic incentive, this solidarity extended beyond the Arab circle to other producers as well, but even here where agreement was easier to obtain than on the boycott issue, there were differing opinions, and Saudi Arabia emerged as the principal dissenter. The Saudi representative tried to soften the price-hiking resolutions of the December 1973 Teheran conference and subsequently attempted to brake OPEC's tendency to proclaim further price boosts.

In fact, these different approaches produced a degree of strain in Saudi-Iranian relations. The respective stands of Saudi Arabia and Iran derive from the vastly different conditions of the two countries. Iran, with a population of around 30 million and with a fast-growing cadre of technocrats and entrepreneurs, is anxious to develop rapidly for political as well as economic reasons. A neighbor of the Soviet Union, Iran is aiming at a standard of living for its masses that would make them immune to the appeal of Communist ideology. Moreover, its government cannot easily forget the trauma of the upheaval during the days of Premier Mossadegh in the early 1950s and is resolved to remove the causes for such would-be dissidence by a determined nationalist policy.

Iran's position on prices is the most forceful of all the OPEC countries. Iran advocates a single world price of oil to be differentiated only by the geographical location and by the quality of the crude produced. This price should be close to that of the closest energy substitute, and, on the other hand, should be subject to determination in accordance with the inflated prices of the industrial and agricultural commodities which Iran, along with other developing countries, is obliged to import. Iran's government denies that it is indifferent to the financial difficulties experienced by the developed West and the less-developed nations as a result of the high oil prices. It points to its own imaginative program of aid and trade, which entails the commitment of $7 billion to a number of countries on a total current revenue of about $21 billion this year.

Saudi Arabia's position and approach are different from those of Iran and some of the other Arab nations. This desert kingdom, with a population about one-fifth or one-sixth that of Iran, has a limited capacity to absorb the influx of oil revenue. It could exist and develop at a reasonable pace either with greatly reduced production or with lower prices. Its government is not anxious to see a collapse of Western economies and the corresponding weakening of the West's defenses against communism. Hence, it favors moderation on the price issue.

These differences between two major oil-producing countries, one Arab and the other non-Arab, are illustrative of the fissures, actual or potential, in the facade of solidarity among the OPEC nations. In addition to these pressures, there are certain forces outside of OPEC that are also likely to exert influence upon its collective decisions. For example, Egypt, a moderate producer but not yet a significant exporting country, appears to gear its oil policies to two considerations: (1) the overall Arab oil strategy connected with the Arab-Israeli conflict and (2) a serious commitment to develop its own oil resources with maximum speed and efficiency. The first consideration has dictated a flexible policy of, first, advocating the Arab oil boycott and, later—following the successful conclusion of disengagement agreements with Israel—urging the discontinuance of the boycott as no longer necessary. The second consideration has led Egypt to favor the presence of American oil companies and to encourage them through a policy of wide-ranging land and offshore concessions. (Incidentally, I see here today representatives of the American corporations that have a stake in the development of oil resources of Egypt.) Egypt's policy appears currently to give high priority to improved relations with the United States and the government's attitudes toward oil questions are appropriate to that objective.

The two oil crises of production and prices have had a mutually reinforcing effect upon worldwide oil transactions. Both have tended to politicize these transactions—that is, to transfer them increasingly from the economic into the political sphere. The transfer has occurred on several levels and in several sectors. In the producing states, it has heightened the awareness of benefits of collective action and the need for solidarity. In the consuming countries, it has spurred government-sponsored search for substitutes to oil and has led governments to assume a more active role in regulating prices, allocating supplies, and planning for all sorts of short- and long-range contingencies. Project Independence in the United States illustrates this trend. Furthermore, partly in response to public nervousness about the oil shortages, punitive legislation against the oil companies was suggested often in disregard of the fact that the shortages really stemmed from foreign political complications.

In their relations with the producing countries, the consumer states faced the alternative of choosing either bilateral or collective approaches. When the Arab oil boycott was at its height, the spirit of "scramble" gripped the policy makers of certain industrial states heavily dependent on foreign oil imports, and this led them toward bilaterality.

Foremost among countries seeking bilateral accommodation was France which concluded with Saudi Arabia and Iran special agreements guaranteeing France substantial oil supplies in return for industrial goods and services involving advanced technology. These included nuclear plants for Iran, nuclear-powered tankers for Saudi Arabia, and a range of similarly sophisticated products. Less evident was the bilaterality practiced by Britain and Japan.

During the winter and early spring of 1974, bilaterality was viewed with concern by the oil companies and with disapproval by official Washington, but for somewhat different reasons. To the oil companies, this sort of bilaterality was symptomatic of the unwelcome trend of government-to-government oil deals, arrangements that actually or potentially reduced the companies' role in international oil transactions and ominously resembled the barter deals signed at one time or another between certain oil producers and the countries of the Communist bloc. The spread of this type of transaction into the capitalist West implied "creeping socialism" and would undermine free enterprise and the efficient mechanism of reliably supplying oil to the markets. The oil companies occasionally asked a pointed question: "If you as a consumer want to be sure of reliable supplies of oil over a specified period of time, who would you trust more readily in concluding a delivery agreement—the government of revolutionary Arab country X, or multinational oil company X, whose freedom from political motivation in supplying its customers and whose diversity of sources of crude are established facts?"

As for official Washington, bilaterality, whether practiced or merely attempted by the Europeans and others, was regarded as highly undesirable, because it introduced unhealthy competition at a time when the maximum cooperation among the consumers was thought to be needed. Therefore, the United States tried to counter the bilaterality with a hurriedly called consumer governments' conference in the early part of 1974. In terms of tangible results, the conference produced a dubious outcome because of two flaws: too little time was devoted to its thorough diplomatic preparation, and too much reliance was placed on America's power of persuasion at that particular juncture of international politics.

Indeed, at that time Washington was not the best venue for a conference of this sort. Only a short time earlier the United States had been designated by the Arab governments as a hostile country to which full embargo was applied. To many Eastern Hemisphere governments, who during and after the October War did their utmost to dissociate themselves from American policy, it appeared risky or outright undesirable to rush to Washington to join in a collective action that the Arabs might interpret as inimical to them. And France, again stressing national self-interest, stood in the forefront of the doubters, delayed its agreement to participate in the conference, and upon eventually appearing, did so with far-reaching reservations. Under the circumstances, the conference produced little beyond the agreement to set up working groups to study various aspects of the situation.

Further, it is noteworthy that the United States itself did not fully renounce bilaterality. When a high-ranking Saudi delegation came to Washington in June 1974, it concluded with the U.S. government an agreement providing for wide-ranging cooperation in the fields of industrialization, technology and science, agriculture, and management. Four joint task forces were created to lay foundations for modernization of Saudi Arabia, and major American research organizations and industrial firms were engaged to produce designs and assist in the development of various sectors of Saudi economy. Not only were these services to be paid for from the rapidly accumulating Saudi dollar surpluses, but also the Saudi government, in helpful response to pleas from the secretary of the treasury, agreed to purchase a substantial amount of U.S. government bonds, thus easing Washington's balance-of-payments liquidity difficulties.

Of course, bilaterality of this sort was different from the strict oil-for-goods deals concluded with the Europeans. There was cash payment for American services and goods and no specific commitment on oil deliveries. Yet the good will and interdependence generated by this kind of major agreement could not, in practical terms, be isolated from the domain of oil, particularly in view of the fact that among major U.S. oil suppliers, Saudi Arabia already held and was bound to hold in the future the most prominent place.

Yet, in spite of this one venture into bilaterality—which, by the way, was viewed with some misgiving in Iran—Washington did not abandon its search for collective action. In late September 1974 it was revealed that, under Washington's prodding, the consuming countries had reached a definite understanding on the twin problems of prices and mutual assistance in the event of new shortages. The fact that an agreement was attained this time could be attributed to two factors. First, the high prices of oil, which raised the specter of the collapse of the West European and Japanese economies, provided a better focus for harmony than did the previous, exclusively Arab oil boycott, which many Europeans attributed to erroneous American foreign policy. Second, the politicizing of oil brought the matter into a sphere in which the old and tested patterns of international politics could be freely imitated.

With vital decisions being made by the governments rather than by the companies, and with the producing governments forming an alliance, was it not inevitable that a counter-alliance of the consumers should come into being sooner or later? And did not the producing governments encourage the transfer of oil matters from the commercial to the political sphere through their government-to-

51

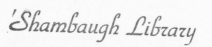

government deals? How long, under these circumstances, could they expect the consuming camp to remain scattered and disorganized? It is true that the consumers' coalition is not perfect and that at this time, as at the time of the earlier Washington conference, France has voiced strong reservations, if not actual dissent. Yet one or two voices of disagreement, even if substantial, cannot arrest what appears to be a law of politics: an action does produce a reaction.

The two coalitions are vastly different from each other. One is composed of states that are militarily weak and less developed but which can muster, by drawing upon their partly colonial past, some convincing moral arguments in their favor. The other represents the highly developed and strong countries whose dependence on imported energy and whose consequent vulnerability have been made suddenly visible. There is a danger of confrontation between the two groups; there is a possibility that some words spoken in the West might be misconstrued as threats to use force. Under the circumstances, the most desirable approach seems to be a negotiated agreement that would take into account, on the one hand, the legitimate interests of the producers with their special needs for development, and, on the other, the imperative of economic—hence, also political—survival of those member-states of the industrial world that depend overwhelmingly on foreign oil imports. Such a rational agreement can best be achieved through quiet diplomacy, without the fanfare of openly taken positions and the resulting vicious circle of rigidity and face-saving. The task is not easy. Indeed, it is the collective character of current actions in both camps that makes discreet diplomacy so difficult.

And yet, there is no alternative to quiet diplomacy if traumatic confrontations are to be avoided. One should not forget that the two camps—the producers and the consumers—have, after all, much in common. Both are located within the free world—that is, outside the Communist orbit—and both have a vital stake in remaining there, enjoying independence and developing their national genius and creative powers free of totalitarian dictation from outside. In this common destiny, both camps can materially help each other, and it certainly is not in the interest of either to see the other go under.

CONGRESSMAN RUPPE: Thank you very much, Professor Lenczowski.

Your thesis is certainly somewhat different from the one that was enunciated this morning. It would appear from your observations that future negotiations will be conducted not so much on an economic basis, perhaps, as on a political basis. I am impressed by your suggestion that this would have to result in negotiated agreements that recognize the legitimate interests of the producers, with their special need for development, and the imperatives of nations dependent on oil for their economic base. Perhaps we could get an observation as to whether your thesis is one that is accepted by the individuals here in this room and also whether such a negotiation might be conducted on a nation-to-nation basis, or will it be undertaken on a user-to-producer—a Western bloc vis-à-vis OPEC—basis?

PROFESSOR LENCZOWSKI: As I pointed out in my presentation, there is a choice between bilaterality and collective action. I think there are great temptations for some states to engage in bilaterality, but it seems to me that, whether we like it or not, collective action will sooner or later become inevitable, as long as collective action is in evidence on one side, as long as the OPEC countries have a coalition—or call it cartel, if you wish to use an economic term.

I look at OPEC as a coalition or an alliance rather than as a cartel because I view the situation in political terms. It is an alliance that is motivated, of course, by economic considerations, because it is not merely an Arab alliance; it includes non-Arab Iran, Venezuela, Indonesia, Canada, and Nigeria. In other words, it is much more than an Arab sphere. I think that here, very often, we commit a mistake by oversimplifying it, and thereby attribute to OPEC certain political motivations that are not there. We tend to confuse the Arab-Israeli issue that relates only to one crisis and one action with elements of the other crisis, the price crisis.

Regardless of other likes and dislikes and preferences, some collective action is inevitable, simply because of laws of politics: one coalition produces another coalition. This is something that is happening and is going to happen. It may not work perfectly; there may be some dissenters; but, nevertheless, I think that it is inevitable.

HENDRIK HOUTHAKKER, Harvard University: I want to question the need for bilateral negotiation between a bloc of producers and a bloc of consumers— the idea which you presented that the coalition of one side will necessarily lead to a coalition on the other side. That is not what you meant by bilateral—I am using it in a different sense now.

Has that been the experience in other commodity agreements? After all, OPEC is very much like many previous attempts to join producers of various commodities—coffee, tin, wheat, and quite a few others. Have you found that there has been a tendency towards coalitions on both sides?

PROFESSOR LENCZOWSKI: Let me say, first of all, that I am not an authority and cannot speak with great knowledge about other commodities. Not being an economist, I have only a rather vague layman's notion about other commodities, combination cartels, prices, and so on.

I look upon oil as a unique commodity, altogether different from tin or what have you. It is a commodity, to be sure, but it is one that has a much greater significance than others, both to its producers and to its consumers. For example, a number of the producing countries just would not be what they are today without oil. How could Iran engage in the experiment known as the White Revolution without the big revenues that are available for such a wholesale social, economic, and cultural transformation? How could we speak of modernization of Saudi Arabia—or of the weapons in the Arab-Israeli struggle—without oil? All of this gives oil very special political overtones and differentiates it from any other commodity except perhaps gold. I just don't consider it as comparable to any other commodity and subject to the same laws.

And as for the consuming countries, our very civilization of today is built upon oil. We speak of further oil discoveries or of the development of substitute sources of energy, but let us be brutally frank with ourselves and acknowledge that for the next ten years there is no substitute for oil in the normal functioning of the civilization we know. Our pattern of living, our standard of living, our production, our employment, our comfort—all depend on oil and its products. Perhaps, after ten years, we may develop some other sources.

If we count, let's say, two to two-and-a-half million barrels a day from Alaska and three million barrels a day from the North Sea—as you see, I am not so sanguine about the North Sea as some Amsterdam professors appear to be—or even six million barrels a day from the North Sea, it is still not going to make that much of a difference in our dependence on OPEC countries, because our consumption is rising by about 5 percent a year. Without oil, we would have to make very major readjustments in the whole pattern of our civilized life, and that is why oil is different.

In addition, as Mr. Levy pointed out so justly before lunch, when you produce a barrel of oil for eighteen cents and sell it for $10.00, obviously, it is not an economic matter but rather a matter of political decision. That political decision can be reached only if there are sovereign governments in combination with each other to make this decision.

PROFESSOR HOUTHAKKER: Let me mention one commodity that may not be quite as crucial to civilization, but about which you could make many of the same statements. There have been many attempts at international wheat agreements; most of them haven't amounted to very much, and finally they collapsed altogether. Why wouldn't the same thing happen to oil agreements?

PROFESSOR LENCZOWSKI: I am not trying to contend that the OPEC coalition is impregnable. It is indeed the lesson of history that coalitions do sometimes splinter away. There are the kind of fissures to which I have referred, and these may indeed develop into very major gaps affecting the survival of a given coalition. I grant you that. I am not absolutely sold on the idea that OPEC is impregnable.

REZA FALLAH, National Iranian Oil Company: Mr. Chairman, having known Professor Lenczowski for some years, I fully expected his very informative and very instructive talk.

I would like to remind him that last February, I think, OPEC opened its doors to a dialogue with the consuming governments. This idea was conveyed in a communiqué which we issued from Vienna last February, and I was party to the drafting of that communiqué. Our intention was to begin a dialogue perhaps with OECD or with the consuming governments concerning the points being discussed today.

But, surprisingly, there was no response whatsoever from the consumers. Instead, a meeting of the consumers was convened—the energy conference in Washington—which did more harm, as far as I can see, than good. To the best of my knowledge, this is the only round table where I have seen representatives of two producing governments present—Ambassador Al-Sabah and Ambassador Zahedi.

Do you not agree that this sort of dialogue—that coordination and cooperation between the two sides, rather than the confrontation which has been the order of the day—would help both sides to understand and appreciate each others' problems, that dialogue is what has been completely lacking in the past year, and the sooner it is begun, the better it will be for both sides?

PROFESSOR LENCZOWSKI: I am grateful for Dr. Fallah's remarks. I had the privilege of conversing with His Majesty, the Shah of Iran about three or four weeks ago in Teheran, and he stressed precisely the point about the readiness of his country to converse. Even when he referred to the price level, he used the word "sliding," meaning movement both up and down, but linking it, of course, to the level of commodity prices. In other words, I must acknowledge that there was a readiness for a dialogue in your country on the highest levels.

ARDESHIR ZAHEDI, Government of Iran: We have, many times, officially brought to the attention of the Western countries, the United States, our willingness to discuss the oil situation on behalf of our own country, and we have pointed out to our friends that confrontation will not get us anywhere.

This is why we suggested many months ago in Rome that representatives of the consumer countries and the producer countries, the Arab world countries, should meet and discuss the oil problem to see what could be resolved.

SALEM AL-SABAH, Government of Kuwait: I support what my brother Ambassador Zahedi said. We went to the United Nations last September in the hope that we could work out an adjustment in the prices not only of oil, but of other commodities. We still are optimistic that the United Nations will find a formula for all commodities.

55

But I would like to refer to the point Professor Lenczowski mentioned about Mr. Levy's talk this morning—that oil prices are politically determined. I would say that oil prices are based on economics more than on politics. As you know, oil is a depletive commodity and some countries, Kuwait for example, are very dependent on their oil resources. We ought to receive the maximum benefit from that commodity in order to maintain the standard of living which we have and to assure a better future for coming generations. Price, therefore, is both an economic and a political matter.

PROFESSOR LENCZOWSKI: I think that basically we are in agreement. I pointed out in my main presentation that the price crisis had an economic origin in contrast to the production crisis, which was Arab-initiated because of the Arab-Israeli war, and was political in origin. The maximization of revenue on the part of the oil-producing countries is an economic consideration.

At the same time, what is important in this crisis with an economic origin is that the decisions are made by sovereign governments. As decisions of sovereign governments, they are in themselves political in character.

It is not the market mechanism that is determining price; rather, price is being set by governments that cooperate with each other through OPEC and adhere to certain policies. The motivation may be economic; the decision was made through political agencies, because every government is a political agency whose decision making is part of the political process.

HERBERT STEIN, University of Virginia: I don't understand, on the basis of Professor Lenczowski's view of the situation, what the two parties will talk about when they sit down to have this dialogue. One party is in control of a commodity which is apparently indispensable to the survival of the other party. When the parties confer, is it possible for them to reach a joint agreement on how rich the one party should be?

It does not seem to me that it is a proper subject for negotiation. If this is an economic question, a question of maximizing income, the producers do not need to discuss it with anybody else. They just need to look at Professor Houthakker's table or at their own version of it. That is a unilateral decision so I wonder what you think the dialogue would be about.

Of course, we have been saying this is too pessimistic a view. But, still, I wonder what are the terms of the dialogue when you put this matter in a political arena and when we who need this indispensable commodity sit down to talk with those who've got it.

PROFESSOR LENCZOWSKI: A number of the producing countries are not indifferent to what happens to the economies and, therefore, to the stability and the political and, ultimately, military strength of some of the Western countries.

For example, I don't think that certain oil-producing countries would be completely indifferent to the collapse of the Italian economy or to a Communist takeover of Italy and the establishment of a Communist state in the very middle of the Mediterranean. I doubt that Iran, which is linked to the West through various defense agreements, including the 1959 bilateral security agreement with the United States and CENTO, is indifferent to what happens to the strength of the West. Nor is Saudi Arabia indifferent to the fate of, let's say, the United States which protected it rather effectively against subversion and aggression during the Yemen civil war when it was being bombed by aircraft from Egypt.

There are a number of political considerations of this kind that can be brought into play if the atmosphere is one of dialogue and good will, and not one of threats. Threats do sometimes produce results, but the longer we can talk to each other in a civilized way, the more convincing, perhaps, we may become to each other.

In other words, I do not believe that the producing countries—although they are acting in their national self-interest and trying to become richer—will necessarily follow short-sighted policies geared to the quick accumulation of currency that could become worthless. There are still many points upon which rational men can find a common ground for agreement. I have not given up hope that this is possible.

WALTER LEVY, Walter Levy and Associates: Let me start off by going back to the Washington energy conference, which was ill-timed and not too well-conceived. I guess I am the only one present who was a participant in that conference. Fundamentally, it went exceedingly well, because, except for France, there was agreement among all countries that participated, and nobody expected Jobert to agree to anything anyhow. The present agreement on emergency sharing (and 145 other points that are included) is now in front of us as a direct result of that conference and has some important political value.

Dr. Fallah, Ambassador Zahedi, and the ambassador from Kuwait are quite right in saying that OPEC has for a long time indicated an interest in discussing energy problems with consuming countries, and the ambassador from Kuwait is quite right to note that the UN meeting was called to encourage discussion. But one problem has been that the importing or consuming countries have been a very disorganized group of countries. Before they are able to talk with any group that is well organized, such as OPEC, there has to be some agreement on what the problem is and on the subjects that should be discussed as a group. After all, OPEC did not invite OECD to join discussions in 1960 or between 1960 and 1970, the formulative period of OPEC, when it was still reasonably powerless. The OPEC countries argued for ten years to get an increase of six cents a barrel in revenue. I think that it took ten years to get this increased revenue. No consuming country was invited to these discussions if I remember correctly.

Another problem is that there is no silent diplomacy possible within the framework of the UN. There is voting, but voting very often, I am afraid to say, without meaningful political content.

Further, at the first sign that the consuming countries were trying to organize themselves, some of the producing countries said, "This is war. If you do organize, that means confrontation." That is not very helpful. And on our side, we have largely accepted the view that any organization of consuming countries toward anything more than matching OPEC in its bargaining and negotiating ability and capability is confrontation.

Finally, let me make a comment on the economics of this problem. Our country is now trying to reduce the demand for oil, if for no other reason than to reduce the balance-of-payments gap. Many other countries will follow suit. But, let me quote a comment of a very prominent petroleum minister from the Middle East: "Of course, the oil prices are not political prices. They are subject to the laws of supply and demand. Which means, that if the demand goes down, we cut supplies." [Laughter.]

That is exactly what was said. I quoted verbatim. With this kind of economic and political philosophy, there is a lot to talk about—and a lot to disagree about.

In the final analysis, of course, nobody could possibly win in a confrontation— by sweat or by force. We had better compromise, or we will suffer more. That means it is not a matter of sweet reason and long-term welfare; it is a matter of awareness of where one's limitations are.

CONGRESSMAN RUPPE: Thank you very much. I have been asked to pose this question: How much time does the world have to work out the arrangements between producers and consumers that a number of you people have suggested, in light of the size and nature of the current international capitals flow?

PROFESSOR HOUTHAKKER: As you may have gathered, I, again, take a cheerful view of things. [Laughter.] Although I have noted some of our most respected leaders making dire predictions of world collapse, I don't really think that is upon us, yet. I believe that the banking system has so far done fairly well in handling the very large flow of capital that has gone around the world.

The main difficulty, as far as I can see, is that some of the oil-producing countries, especially those that are unable to spend the revenues themselves, haven't really come to any policy yet as to what they will do with these vast funds, and, therefore, they have gone in a seemingly arbitrary fashion from one place to put their funds to another. This has been somewhat disturbing.

The Eurodollar market is a mechanism that is already quite large—and, in my opinion, well equipped to deal with these flows. I don't think that the financial element is the main reason for coming to an agreement in the near future. The dangers of a collapse of the world financial system, I think, are still fairly remote. If there are problems in the international financial system, they are only partly related to the oil problem. They are probably more related to the inability of many banks to adjust to a regime of floating rates, the temptation of speculation, and things of that kind.

The oil money, itself, I believe, has not been a major destabilizing factor— and isn't going to be, in part, because the Arab countries, who are the ones who accumulate the funds, generally have a history of very conservative financial management. There is no indication, fortunately, that the Arab oil producers are even considering using this money in a destabilizing fashion. That is why I think the financial factor is not the one which we should be most concerned about. The financial dangers are much exaggerated, in my opinion.

CONGRESSMAN RUPPE: Mr. Stein, would you care to make an observation on that point?

PROFESSOR STEIN: I agree with Henk that we are not going to have a collapse, although, perhaps, for a somewhat different reason. I am not quite so sure about the adequacy of the existing private financial institutions, but I think that in the end there are enough sound and financially strong governments around—particularly us—to bail out those who get into the most difficulty.

I suppose, although you can't be sure with the way our political process works, that in the crunch we would bail them out. But what I get out of this kind of discussion is that there is a kind of race or contest between us and the oil-producing countries about who cares most whether the Italians go Communist.

That is what Professor Lenczowski seems to see as a limitation on the demands of the oil-producing countries—their great unwillingness to see the Italians and some others go Communist. And I think the limitation on our hard line about foreign aid is set by our unwillingness to see the Italians go Communist. We don't want to stand ready to bail the Italians out too early, because we want to put some pressure both on the Italians and on the oil-producing countries to avoid pushing the Italians and others into that kind of abyss. We may have a kind of game of chicken here, in which somebody might not get up in time one morning to keep the Italians from going Communist. But I don't think that is going to happen.

I think there is a basis for talk between the producers and consumers, but I think it lies in the kind of thing that Henk was saying this morning: if there isn't some relief on the price side, the rest of the world will make enormous investments in the development of substitute forms of energy and substitute ways of living that don't involve so much use of energy. In the end we will have spent tens or hundreds of billions of dollars in that process, ending with the oil in the ground in the Middle East being worth much less than it might otherwise have been and leaving us all worse off than if the oil had been sold more cheaply, and we had not made all those investments in alternative energy sources. This seems to me to be the economic basis of a discussion between the two parties.

AMBASSADOR ZAHEDI: As Professor Lenczowski has mentioned, we are certainly interested, we are actually part of the world in which we are living. Certainly, we are interested in seeing that, for instance, Italy, France or England not go bankrupt or Communist. If we were not interested, we would not have committed ourselves to more than $8 billion dollars in aid to other countries. And in November we are having the president of Italy as our guest in Iran. One of the things we are going to discuss is the economy of his country.

I think these and other things show how much we are willing to cooperate and how much we care for the future of other nations. But we must remember that the prices of some other commodities have jumped more than 300 and in some cases more than 400 percent in the last ten years.

There is no question that we have only a limited amount of time in order to find a solution. I believe that we have already achieved much just in the last few hours of our meeting here. This is a demonstration of the better results to be expected through talking than through confrontation. What would be the results of confrontations? Could gunboat diplomacy get anywhere today? The need is for cooperation, and my country has said we are ready to get together. Speaking not only for my country, but for the OPEC countries, I can say that we have always been willing to hold discussions with consumers.

Of course, it is up to the consuming countries whether they would like to have a confrontation or not. The OPEC countries have already said we are ready to get together. At the same time, we cannot accept the whatever is mine is mine and whatever is yours is negotiable approach. If we want to get together, and if we have good will, I am sure we will be able to come out with a good result for all. I am personally optimistic. I think we will be able to solve the problem— as long as we have understanding from both sides.

CONGRESSMAN RUPPE: One question that has been posed is, what is the interest of Soviet Russia in all this? Is the policy of the Soviet Union likely to be directed toward dividing the producers and the consumers, or is it likely to be a policy of splitting up the consumer and producing blocs?

PROFESSOR LENCZOWSKI: I believe that the Soviet Union has thus far been kept largely out of the whole political-economic problem of oil, because the Soviet Union, together with its bloc, is by and large self-contained insofar as oil is concerned.

The U.S.S.R. is an exporter; it has reserves; it has made some very important discoveries, especially recently, and perhaps it may emerge, therefore, as an exporter on a larger scale. But thus far we can still deal with international oil problems without bothering too much about the role of the Soviet Union.

We have to take into account, of course, the Soviet role in penetrating the Middle East. In a study I wrote about a year-and-a-half ago on Soviet advances in the Middle East, I did make some investigation into what the Soviets are doing in the field of oil. In Egypt they have not done very much. In Iraq they have stepped into a breach created by the deterioration of relations between the Western oil companies and Iraq.

But by and large, the Soviet role has not been prominent in international oil politics. I would say that it may become prominent if Soviet petroleum discoveries lead to such a production that the Soviet Union could and would want to become a major exporter.

It is worth noting that the U.S.S.R. as an exporter has benefited greatly from the rise in prices. Soviet benefits from the collective OPEC action—in which the Soviets did not participate, but just reaped benefits—have been estimated at $7 billion. Thus the Soviet Union, without too much effort, found itself in possession of disposable liquidity in hard currency, which she may use for whatever purpose she considers useful to her national or ideological interests.

Undoubtedly, this is a fact that we cannot completely disregard in these discussions, and I would say that the oil-producing countries should not disregard it either. Iran—a country close to the Soviet Union—or any other oil-producing country that is not favorably disposed to the Soviet Communist system might give some thought to this particular factor.

JOHN NASSIKAS, Federal Power Commission: I'd like to address this to Dr. Lenczowski, if I may.

First, to what extent do you believe that the OPEC nations' policies on solidarity may be influenced by member-nation attitudes toward Israel? Second, to what extent are the consuming nations destined to be polarized in order to pay for an unfavorable balance of trade as the result of monopolistic world prices that bear no relationship to economic costs?

PROFESSOR LENCZOWSKI: Well, sir, as regards the issue of solidarity, I believe—and I mention it briefly in my main presentation—I believe that the solidarity of the price issue was easier to achieve for the OPEC nations than a solidarity on the boycott issue. First of all, the boycott or production cutback issue was really a purely Arab affair in which Iran, Indonesia, Venezuela, and Nigeria were not involved. Generally speaking, I am still inclined to think that the price issue is not connected too much with the Arab-Israeli issue, although, if we make too much noise about it on the consuming side, we may perhaps give some ideas to at least the Arab component of OPEC to consider that indeed the price is also a weapon to be used as the cutbacks in production were used. We have it in our power to create those adverse reactions in the Arab world that may lead the Arabs to review their policy with the idea of using price as a political weapon.

However, I don't think it has been so far; in fact, I would say that the Arabs were rather riding the coat-tails of Iran on the price issue. Iran initiated this move at the Teheran conference, and Iran has been the most forceful spokesman and proponent of keeping prices high and adjusting them to the prices of commodities. The most important Arab country, Saudi Arabia, has had a very reserved view about this, and other Arab countries have followed—including Saudi Arabia eventually—the Iranian leadership on this, but without the same forcefulness.

As regards your question on the consuming nations: It's a hypothetical question, because it is really asking how will these Western nations, including France, Britain, Italy, Germany, and ourselves really react? Governments have different senses of urgency and face different economic situations. Some economies are stronger and some weaker. And the corresponding political situations in these countries vary. I believe that if the terrific drain of hard currency continues for a long time, bringing tremendous changes and adjustments in the economic, political, and social life of the consuming countries, there will inevitably be a strong demand to take a stand that will lead to some sort of cooperation. Indeed, as has been mentioned several times during this discussion, this cooperation is already gradually being created.

MR. NASSIKAS: I was thinking of the possibility that the traditional alliances—NATO, the European Common Market—might deteriorate.

PROFESSOR LENCZOWSKI: I think there are definite political dangers in each nation going it alone.

AMBASSADOR AL-SABAH: I agree with what my brother Ardeshir Zahedi of Iran said. We also wish to enter into discussions with good will. The fact that we are here as officials of our governments shows that we are ready to talk in order to find a settled price for this commodity and for other commodities.

It cannot be said that we are not participating in developing other nations and helping other nations to survive. The Kuwait Development Fund, with $12 billion in loans guaranteed by the government, invests not only in the Arab states but also in Africa and Asia. I think the thing is how we cooperate and work together. We have the capital; we lack some experience, some know-how. We welcome the help of the most advanced countries to come and participate with us. There is no problem of how to invest our money and how to handle it. I think the thing is how we cooperate and work together.

GWEN MURPHREE, League of Women Voters: It would seem from the discussion thus far that the politics of world oil is concerned only with consuming nations and producing nations. Would you comment on the needs of developing countries in this whole picture of world politics, Professor Lenczowski?

PROFESSOR LENCZOWSKI: Very obviously if oil prices continue to be as high as they are, and if the underdeveloped countries do not get some kind of a compensation for these high oil prices one way or another—either by aid from oil-producing countries, which would have to be administered very wisely and properly spread, or by the aid from the industrial countries that traditionally have been trying to extend assistance to them—then they are going to face tremendous difficulties bordering on catastrophe.

It's a tremendous problem, and it is comforting to see that countries like Iran and Kuwait have already committed funds to a number of underdeveloped countries. The needs of underdeveloped countries are tremendous. Certainly, India's difficulties are great, but we may note that Iran has committed nearly $1 billion for India. And there is $2 billion pledged to Afghanistan, the motivation, I think, being mixed, both economic and political, to save Afghanistan from some worse fate following its revolution last year.

I think it's feasible, it's possible to help these and other countries. The problem is, how systematic will this aid be? Will there be some great gaps left unfilled?

I think I answered your question. And now I want to make one comment regarding the collective action that was raised both by Mr. Levy and Ambassador Al-Sabah of Kuwait. Mr. Levy, you mentioned the objections of the producing countries to collective action by Western countries. My understanding was that these loud objections to collective Western action were largely voiced at the time of the oil boycott. It was not so much over the price issue. It was primarily the Arabs who raised their voices very strongly against any possible combination and mutual help of Western countries at the time of embargoes and cutbacks, because the Arab policy at that time was a discriminating policy, an attempt to differentiate between hostile countries, friendly countries, neutral countries, and so forth. And the Arabs were very uneasy about the fact that a country that might find itself on their embargo list would be receiving by backdoor from other countries, through collective action of mutual help, oil supplies that were not supposed to be reaching that country.

Consequently, the Arabs were extremely sensitive on the issue of collective action. I think that today, when the matter has shifted from oil boycott to oil price and from the Arab community to the general OPEC community, the situation is different, and I see much more willingness for a dialogue and, in fact, virtual acceptance of the inevitability that the West will organize itself.

MELVIN R. LAIRD, *Reader's Digest* and the AEI National Energy Project: Congressman Phil Ruppe has an important vote coming up on the floor of the

63

House of Representatives, and will have to leave us now. Thanks for being with us, Phil. [Applause.]

We'll now continue the discussion.

JOHN ANTHONY, Johns Hopkins University: It seems to me that you have been—perhaps justifiably—pessimistic about the prospects for a meaningful dialogue between the producers and the consumers. Do you think that a genuinely meaningful dialogue might not develop, perhaps, as Ambassador Zahedi has suggested, involving a linkage between oil prices and the prices of other commodities?

PROFESSOR STEIN: Well, I didn't really mean to express a negative attitude toward the dialogue. I was trying to find out what the dialogue would be about.

I know what we would say in a dialogue. We'd say, "We'd like to see the price lower." Now, what would they say and what would be the variables that would be on the table when we have this dialogue?

As for escalators, I have no objection to that. I'm inclined to favor a much more widespread escalation than we've now got on a lot of commodity prices, and I don't see any objection to escalating the price of oil.

My only question is where you escalate from? If you escalate it from $10.00, it's different than if you escalate it from $5.00. But I think that could be done unilaterally by the sellers under present circumstances if they wanted to establish an escalated price level, since they seem to determine the price.

I don't want to suggest that I think dialogue is unprofitable. I want to get a little more specific about what we talk about when we get around the table.

VERMONT ROYSTER, University of North Carolina: Not being either an economist or a political scientist, but merely a journalist who has observed both aspects over a period of time, I would like to say that, in a way, we set up an artificial division here in having one session on economics and one on politics. We cannot separate the two, and many times they go around in a circle. It has been my observation that while there are some political issues that are not economic—religious differences, for example—there are really no economic issues that are not political, whether within a country or between countries.

On Herb's point on the question of what the dialogue would be about and what the effect of all of this money going to the oil-producing countries would be, it seems to me there are several points here.

One is strictly political. In the first place, most of these countries—with a few exceptions, but most of them—particularly those in the Middle East, are relatively small countries. They would suffer greatly politically if any action they took resulted in any serious weakening of the Western countries.

As for all of this money going to the oil-producing countries, unless they are going to dig holes in the sand and put this money down in them, something has to be done with it. Now, examples have been given of going to Sierra Leone and other places with aid, but basically they have to use the money to buy goods from the industrial part of the world.

On the economic issue: If the oil-producing countries carry things too far, dig holes in the sand and just sit on the money, they run the risk of causing a monetary collapse of the Western industrialized nations. This would certainly do the oil-producing countries no good. They are paid in dollars, marks, pounds, and so forth. A monetary collapse would make all of their alleged profit vanish. So I think there are many things that can be put on the table.

At some point, the consuming countries, particularly the industrial consuming countries, are almost bound to recognize their common interest. It's almost like the principle in physics where an action has an equal and opposite reaction. In the first days of the oil crisis, the embargo and the price crisis, we really had a panic. In a panic situation, everybody goes running every man for himself. I think we are past that stage now. I think that even countries like France and Japan, which were the two that first ran off by themselves, are beginning to change. I think that we will get to a point where the Western industrial countries, the consuming countries, will see their community of interest and the producing countries will see that they cannot carry their point of view too far.

As a matter of fact—I hate to sound like a Pollyanna—in many ways I'm very glad all of this happened. We were getting into a worldwide monetary inflation long before the oil crisis came along. We were headed in that way and it would have hit us at some point in any event. The oil crisis, which actually had nothing to do with inflation whatever as a monetary phenomenon, so shook us up that this country is really in favor of some medicine for our own internal inflation situation. I don't think this would have happened for another five years if it hadn't been for the oil crisis. So that is a plus value. I suspect you're going to find now that, if the Western industrialized, consuming countries can begin to see a commonality of interest in terms of the energy problem, you will begin to see that transferred into another area—namely, some sort of a decent international monetary and currency market by agreement of some sort.

So I have a feeling that things aren't as bad as some of the conversation around the table would lead us to believe. Sometimes, in domestic politics anyway, things have to get worse before they can get any better. They have to get so much worse that everybody recognizes that you've got to do something about it. And this is what I think is happening and has been happening since the oil embargo and the price crisis. I'm really glad to have a crisis, because the crisis will make us go to the doctor.

JOHN LICHTBLAU, Petroleum Industry Research Foundation, Inc.: Following up on this interaction of politics and economics, Professor Lenczowski was correct when he said that the Arab oil embargo was strictly political action and the price increase was economic action. This is true, but can you really separate those two completely? Isn't there some feedback between them?

I am thinking particularly about the price increase of December 1973. I'll say 70 percent of the price increase occurred in October 1973—you had in December an additional 130 percent increase. And that was taken in the midst of a major oil shortage. In the midst of crisis, with panic buying driving the average market price of oil up to something like 15, 16, $17.00 a barrel. In the OPEC discussions in December 1973, it was pointed out that the posted prices had no relation to market prices. Well, it didn't exactly end up that way, but I do not believe that you would have had an $11.65 posted price, at that time, established by OPEC, if there hadn't been a shortage, if there hadn't been panic buying.

So in a way the current price is a legacy of the Arab-Israeli war and of the use of oil as a strategic weapon in this struggle. We are stuck with it. I can't imagine that there would have been any other reason to jump the price of oil that much. The OPEC nations were never totally unaware of market prices when they set their price in the past. I don't think they would have been unaware of market prices had the market price been $5.00 or $6.00 lower in December 1973. Of course the embargo was ended within a few months, and once the price moved up there was no way of moving it down again. But I think there is an interaction there which has to be taken into account.

PROFESSOR LENCZOWSKI: I'm glad you are raising this point. Let me answer by stressing two things. First of all, at the very beginning of my presentation, when referring to the two crises and their different origins, I said, "Moreover, although the two crises have different origins, one political and the other economic, they became conceptually interconnected in that a price regulation would have been impossible to achieve without the demonstrated ability to control production."

Obviously. But as to the second point—whether the Arab-Israeli conflict has specifically affected the price rise—this is a very controversial question, because there will be certain Arabs—and I have talked to many—who would agree with the proposition that actually the price hike was counterproductive to the basic Arab oil strategy of cutbacks, of penalizing foes and rewarding friends. With the price increase, everybody is hit and whatever benefit was derived from rewarding friends is lost.

So some Arab observers would agree that this was counterproductive. But there are others who would say that the attitude of Saudi Arabia was very negatively affected by the American commitment of $2.2 billion for Israeli armaments, and that therefore, even though she had misgivings about the price rises, eventually went along. In any case, this is still a somewhat murky area where I think a good deal of research about the facts could be done very profitably.

GEORGE PIERCY, Exxon Corporation: At one time the Iranians said that $7.00 per barrel oil was competitive energy, and that's what Iran would go for. Now we have to go to $11.65 with 55 percent of it tax to give us that. We haven't stopped at $7.00 oil. Now it's between $9.00 and $10.00, and this has come about through the portion of the oil that the governments own and sell.

I think each party in this had some different intentions, but whatever they were, they've got out of hand now.

AMBASSADOR ZAHEDI: First of all, I must say that there is no doubt that this problem is both economic and political. When we held the auction of our oil, it sold for $16.00 to $20.00 per barrel. It was the American companies that came to buy it at this price. To be very honest with you, we never expected that they would pay that high a price. The most we thought we would get was somewhere between $10.00 to $11.00.

Now, one of the questions which was raised here was what are we going to do with all the money? We would love to spend it in the industrial countries to buy the technology and know-how we need. We cannot eat the money, we need to use it in developing our country.

Like Mr. Royster, I am optimistic about the future, but we are probably going to have things worse—for a while—before they become better. I am not really very worried for the United States or for Europe. They will be able to take care of themselves. I am worried about the Third World and the "Fourth World." The Third World is comprised of those countries which at least have something to sell in order to get what they want. The Fourth World, which has more than a billion people in it, has only hunger, disease and drought. We really have to look after and see what we can do for it. How are we going to do it? We can do something with aid from the oil-producing countries, but there is no question that the oil price rise has created problems, because it has been so sudden. We have to find one price. That price would be the price which would tell us as sellers or producers how much we are going to get, and you, as a consumer, how much you are going to pay. Then you could plan a one-year or two-year program for yourselves. If we would be able to come to a price—whether that price would be $7.00 or whether it would be $9.00 or whatever—and say, all right the past is past, and this is the real price of the commodity to be paid today, we would be in one little boat together.

We are willing to talk, that I can assure you. We want to, because we need the friendship of the West; we need the technology of the West; we want to develop our countries. It is not because we are in love with you, it is just because we are in love with ourselves. I think we are as anxious as any of you to be able to solve the problem.

PART FOUR

World Oil and the American Economy

After dinner Alan Greenspan, chairman of the President's Council of Economic Advisers, was questioned about whether oil prices were too high and how much oil price hikes contributed to inflation.

WORLD OIL AND THE AMERICAN ECONOMY

MELVIN R. LAIRD, *Reader's Digest* and the AEI National Energy Project: The President of the United States felt that, as new chairman of his Council of Economic Advisers, he would like to have a man that had great experience with industry. So he decided to send to the Senate of the United States the name of Alan Greenspan.

In the few short weeks he has been in Washington, Alan has learned that the only leaks in government today as far as the ship of state is concerned come from the top of the ship. And he is learning as he becomes involved in the very difficult economic problems that face the United States that politics really is the art and science of government—that economics is important, but that the real decisions as far as this country is concerned are not based upon economic judgments, but upon political judgments.

I introduce to you tonight, to talk to you informally and to respond to your questions, Washington's newest politician, Alan Greenspan, chairman of the President's Council of Economic Advisers.

MR. GREENSPAN: Thank you, Mr. Laird—I think! Now, what's the first question?

MR. LAIRD: What are the most controversial parts of the President's recommendations to the Congress?

MR. GREENSPAN: I find that at this particular stage there is literally no answer that one can give, because anybody who is worth his salt can figure out by the types of nonanswers given what the program is all about. All I will indicate is that there is a program, it is pretty much developed at this stage, and there will be a speech.

HERBERT STEIN, University of Virginia: When is the next program coming out?

MR. GREENSPAN: You are an expert on that. All I can say is that we have done so much work in the last couple of weeks that we have material enough for about five or six programs.

PROFESSOR STEIN: A large inventory?

MR. GREENSPAN: We have a large inventory.

VERMONT ROYSTER, University of North Carolina: I would like to ask you a question about Mel's opening comment about political decisions. How do you see your role as chairman of the Council of Economic Advisers? That is, the President is going to make political decisions. When you are called in to advise the President on any particular issue, do you attempt to find the acceptable political path or do you see your role in some other fashion?

MR. GREENSPAN: Basically, I think that I am most skilled in doing underlying economic and statistical analysis. What I am planning to do is set up a system by which we will be feeding in essentially analytical contributions to the economic decision-making process. It is certainly true that ultimately every economic decision is and must be a political one, but politics does not exist independently of economics, and there are a great number of political decisions which have been bad political decisions because they presuppose something about the economic consequences of certain political decisions. As I see my role, I am to evaluate the economic consequences that I can foresee of various alternate courses, both in the short run and in the long run. The value choices which the President must make are not, obviously, necessarily guided by that, but I do think that those are essential and necessary ingredients.

JOHN ROBERTS, Voice of America: Mr. Greenspan, we had two trial balloons floated today on gasoline taxes, one by Mr. Sawhill's office on the 20 percent surcharge and one by Mr. Laird on the necessity of combining some sort of tax on gasoline with rationing. Which one do you prefer? Or do you favor both? Or neither?

MR. GREENSPAN: What's gasoline? [Laughter.]
I would say at the moment that is not even a meaningful question. There is just no way I can answer except by asking John to come up here, and he looks more tired than I am.

QUESTION: It is generally agreed that part of the economic program to be announced next week will include an energy petroleum conservation measure. What is the goal for the oil consumption cutback—if there is such an element in the program?

MR. GREENSPAN: I cannot answer that in any way whatever without discussing substantive issues. I hate to be evasive, but there's just no way for me not to be evasive on questions like that at this particular time. So, rather than try to give you phony answers, I'll just say I cannot comment.

GEORGE PIERCY, Exxon Corporation: Let me switch from the domestic to the international scene and maybe you will have less trouble, Mr. Greenspan. We spent the day on energy and oil, and we have representatives of two oil-producing countries here. I think they have all convinced us that they are reasonable people and that we should have a dialogue with them. It seems to me that we have not tried to convince the producing governments that today's price of oil, let's say $10.00 or close to $10.00, is too high. How would you go about convincing our oil-producing friends that today's price of oil is too high, if you agree that it is?

MR. GREENSPAN: I agree that it's too high. I think the first question you have to ask yourself is where their self-interest lies. And the answer applies technically over a very long-term context. It's fairly obvious that some major producers are going to have very substantial reserves for a very long period of time, and the optimum price that one could consider, if you're going to maximize your returns, must basically be one which gives you the highest present value. Looking at pricing from that point of view, I think it's necessary for us to convince people that at the current price of oil there will be sufficient expansion in oil supplies over the next five to ten years so that the market price for oil in the future will be low and the present value, in the sense of the reserves at the moment, would be increased if one had a more moderate price that did not cause the types of distortions that exist. Obviously, that is a fairly complex cost-benefit analysis, but I believe it is correct and essentially would be the one, if I were running price policy, that I would get at.

It is clearly an analysis that is very difficult technically to convey. Certainly one problem is that we in the Western world, with our inflations that existed before the oil thing, see sufficient uncertainty and instability in the long-term outlook that it is by no means clear to us that the longer-term price for oil will go down. It's important for us to make what I think is a fairly easy economic forecast credible to the OPEC nations. Now, I must say I do not know how one goes about that at this particular stage. I think it is a terribly complex economic argument. I think it is true, and since it is true, I think we should be able to convey that particular notion to them. But I am glad I do not have to do the job.

RICHARD FAIRBANKS, Ruckelshaus, Beveridge and Fairbanks, and the AEI National Energy Project: Can I ask you another analytic question that follows from the previous question? In analyzing the present inflation in the United States, what percentage do you attribute to the rise in international oil prices in the last eighteen months?

MR. GREENSPAN: It's not easy to estimate it for the following reason: you can get an absolute statistical answer only if you believe that the movements of all prices are essentially independent and that markups exist in the conventional way. You then could use some sort of an input-output system to try to figure out what the price relationship is with and without a huge oil price. The only problem with that method is that the longer-term price pattern is essentially a monetary phenomenon and the average price level in the United States is a function of unit money supply, that is, money supply divided by physical volume. The reason that's significant is that if you literally believed that there is a causal relationship between unit money supply and prices—these have been in extremely close parallel movement for the last several years, and, in fact, for the last fifteen or twenty years—if you literally believed that it was money supply that was causing the rise in the general price level, then one could argue that the increases in international oil prices have nothing whatever to do with the price increase. This argument is not perfect in that some of the increase in money supply in the United States has resulted in an attempt to accommodate sharp increases in oil prices.

What we do know is that the effect of the increase in oil price in the United States lies within some fairly wide boundaries. My suspicion is that it has a significant transitory effect on the U.S. price level, but I think it's probably far less than a lot of the statistical analyses we have seen would indicate. I don't know how much less, but I'm inclined to believe that if the oil price were to flatten out and stay flat indefinitely, we probably wouldn't lose more than a small percentage of our current inflation rate. What I am getting at really is that while the oil price increase has been significant in our price problem, it's been overestimated as a major, underlying element in the inflation of the United States. I'll even go as far as to say it's been overestimated as a factor in world inflation. It's huge, obviously, but I think it's a lot smaller than people make it out to be.

STANLEY BENJAMIN, United Press International: Mr. Greenspan, I would like to get your comment on the basic economic theory of using the private enterprise system to provide essential goods and services, in this case energy. I understand that the Ford administration's position is for free enterprise. But to take a simplified example, Gulf Oil, I think, was talking about buying a circus with its money. The trade-off here, for Gulf, I presume, is that it views the circus as potentially profitable. And if something like a circus, certainly a luxury item, is more profitable than the production of something essential, such as oil, then how does the free enterprise system make sure that the essentials are provided at a reasonable cost that people can afford? Isn't there an incentive to go out and make the most money you can, no matter how you do it and without regard for people's needs?

MR. GREENSPAN: I'm not familiar with the specific example, but let's assume that the hypothesis is correct, that circuses are more profitable than oil—I don't believe they are, but let's take that as given. There are actually other reasons for diversification. What you are essentially telling me is that there are a vast number of people in our society who get considerable enjoyment out of circuses and what these people are doing, in a sense, is just using some of the funds they might have used, say, for gasoline and driving to go to a circus. What we are saying here is that basically what the market system tries to do is to meet the wants of the American people. I think that is the purpose of a free market society.

MR. BENJAMIN: I am not really suggesting that at all. I am suggesting that if an investor or a company can make a larger return on capital investments in some luxury activity, then what is the incentive to put capital into the less profitable activity, which is essential?

MR. GREENSPAN: I am sorry; I am missing your point. Which do you think is the less profitable?

MR. BENJAMIN: Let us say the circus has the higher profit margin.

MR. GREENSPAN: It doesn't, but that's okay.

MR. BENJAMIN: You put in a little money and you get a lot back. Okay, well, let us say oil is vice versa. Now, given this, how does the market provide needed goods and services? The traditional function of the government has been to step in where something is not profitable for private industry and do it—providing services like education and—

MR. GREENSPAN: You are certainly not trying to tell me that oil is not profitable at the moment. But I'm obviously missing the thrust of your question, because clearly, when one diversifies, which is essentially what that sort of activity is, what one is trying to do is to lower the cost of capital for the total enterprise. You diversify the risk, and the basic purpose of doing that is to construct a situation in which capital costs are lower so that all goods and services, if you generalize in this sort of thing, come in at lower cost. In other words, you are lowering the risk premiums in the system by diversifying and you do so in order to maintain a flow of goods and services at the lowest cost.

Does that answer the thrust of your question?

MR. BENJAMIN: Let me just follow it up. What I am getting at is the argument made by the oil companies that they cannot drill for more oil unless they get a higher profit margin—unless they get what they call a better rate of return. They do not say they are losing money; they say they are not making as much money as are other enterprises that compete for the capital. What I am asking here is how should we value this system in which enterprises which are less essential can draw capital away from enterprises which are more essential.

MR. GREENSPAN: But remember that the concept of "essential" presupposes a standard. And the basic question is: a standard in this context largely represents a value to whom?

The issue of what is necessary and what is not necessary, what is essential and not essential, presupposes a human value system. We know, for example, that when confronted with alternate choices, people spend their money in all sorts of peculiar ways which you yourself and perhaps I do not even understand. We know of many cases in which people go out and buy extraordinary things and deprive themselves of all sorts of necessities.

I do not think that it is one aspect of a free society that the government, or the people acting through their representatives, have a right to make those choices for the individual. I think that what we like our market system to do is not to pass judgment from afar as to what types of values individuals should have. It is in the nature of a free society that those value judgments are reflected in the marketplace, and the concept of essential or not essential is something which I think reflects itself in our system. I think that's what is good about it.

QUESTION: This afternoon we had the ambassadors of Kuwait and Iran here at the discussion, and they commented that last February, after the OPEC meeting in Vienna, they sought a dialogue with the then Nixon administration in order to talk about what was coming and what had been, and that they got no response, either from Washington or from any other capital. They said that sitting down here today in this forum represents one of the few beginning steps toward the establishment of this sort of dialogue. Is the Ford administration ready now to undertake such a broad dialogue with the oil-producing countries in an effort to move this whole problem away from confrontation?

MR. GREENSPAN: I am not serving in that particular diplomatic or economic role. I could guess at what the policy intention might be, but I do not think it would be appropriate for me to do so. You are asking me a very specific policy question which is more in John Sawhill's line than it is in mine.

QUESTION: You said that the impact of oil price increases on inflation has been somewhat overrated. How would you rate the impact of the oil price increase upon balance of payments?

MR. GREENSPAN: Oh, I think it has been just extraordinary. All you have to do is take a look at what is happening to the fund flows, but more importantly, we must ponder the debt burden that is being created as a result of these extraordinary flows of funds. The impact upon prices, I think, is less than the statistics suggest. There is no question as to what is happening in the financial system, because while one can envisage the types of flows that go on, in a balance of payments sense, we just look at the net changes.

I do not think we are sufficiently aware of the total implications for most of the oil-importing countries in the world, because it is fairly apparent that these types of flows engender such huge debt equity balance sheet ratios on a consolidated basis that it is very difficult to project these levels of monies going on indefinitely without running into literal arithmetical problems in constructing a world balance sheet system.

QUESTION: First, do you agree with the assessment of Russell Peterson, chairman of the Council on Environmental Quality, that the costs due to environmental controls are only one-half of one percent of the inflation rate?

MR. GREENSPAN: I have not looked at those calculations. The estimate strikes me as a bit low, frankly, but I have not yet been able to look sufficiently closely at the cost effects of environmental controls. Calculations of that kind are extremely difficult to make and require an awful lot of assumptions. I have not really looked at those assumptions, so I couldn't really evaluate Mr. Peterson's estimate.

QUESTION: Do you think we are paying too high a cost, in terms of the inflation rate, for the environmental controls?

MR. GREENSPAN: That is precisely the type of political decision that gentlemen like Secretary Laird can answer.

MR. LAIRD: I'm retired.

QUESTION: The second part of my question then: do you think that, in making its assessments, the CEA should build into its data base the true environmental costs of some of the decisions that may be recommended?

MR. GREENSPAN: Yes—this is the type of thing that we need a great deal more of. I do not think we do sufficient cost-benefit analysis for the vast variety of decisions that are made in our society. There has to be some very major upgrading of the analysis, the economic analysis, of the implications of the political trade-off decisions that we have been making.

ELVIS J. STAHR, National Audubon Society: I think you said, Dr. Greenspan, that the cost of energy, and particularly of foreign oil, is not the only factor in the rapid growth of inflation in the past year. You said it was maybe not as significant as it sometimes is made out to be.

MR. GREENSPAN: But it is significant, obviously.

DR. STAHR: What I am wondering is whether there is going to be great stress—without revealing any details of next Tuesday—on the rather obvious benefits of serious efforts of energy conservation as a means not only of bringing inflation under control but also of getting progress on some of our other problems, like interest rates, pollution, and so on.

MR. GREENSPAN: I do not believe that energy conservation is an unquestioned, unqualified good. In all sorts of analyses, I think it is important to look at the costs of conservation. In other words, conservation is a commodity. And I hope we realize that when we go in one direction, it has other costs. I think what is terribly important is to balance and find the right paths. Those are very rough types of decisions, but they are the types of decisions, I think, that we are going to have to make an awful lot of in the next few years, far more than we have made in the last decade.

DR. STAHR: Let me suggest that the trade-offs are easier there than nearly anywhere else, because cutting out waste produces mostly benefits and not too much cost.

WILLIS D. SMITH, Senate Interior Committee: Are you optimistic or pessimistic? [Laughter.]

MR. LAIRD: Give them a little optimistic forecast.

MR. GREENSPAN: Let me put it this way. I do not know if any of you have seen this, but I thought I had the solution to inflation when I picked up this "Wizard of Id" comic strip which somebody gave me. It shows the King looking at his subjects and his subjects are crying out, "What are you going to do about inflation?" And the King sits there smiling and says, "Print more money." Then the finance minister, with great chagrin on his face, looks in and says, "We can't do that, Sire." And the King says, "Why not?" The finance minister answers, "There is no more gold to back it up." And the King exclaims with obvious relief, "Phew, for a moment there I thought we were out of paper." [Applause.]

MR. LAIRD: We do appreciate your coming over here tonight, Alan. We know that it was a very uncomfortable position for you to be in, in view of the fact that these meetings are going forward and the President is going to address the country with an economic message on Tuesday next.

Our discussions today, I think, have come to one conclusion, and that is that, here in the United States, the time has come for some pretty tough action. I am sure that this country, with the new administration, will be able to mobilize public support for what is best for America, and what is best for America during this period of time is not going to be the easiest for America. Thank you very much. [Applause.]

PART FIVE

Dialogue on World Oil

The panelists and participants in the "Dialogue on World Oil" agreed that the most serious immediate aspect of the world oil problem is the abruptness of the increases in the price of oil before either producing or consuming nations had devised the means for handling and constructively utilizing such large-scale transfers of wealth. The fact that some transfer of wealth would continue was not in dispute. Most of the panelists felt the solution to these problems could be found through a constructive dialogue between producing and consuming nations. Representatives of Saudi Arabia, Iran, and Kuwait invited the consuming nations to organize for such a dialogue, rather than for a confrontation with the producers. At one point, Minister Yamani of Saudi Arabia promised that his country would not cut its oil production in response to decreased demand due to conservation efforts. However, he said that the ingredients for another Middle East war still remained, and if another war were to come, there would be another interruption of the oil supply from the area.

DIALOGUE ON WORLD OIL

MELVIN R. LAIRD, *Reader's Digest* and the AEI National Energy Project: Ladies and gentlemen, this is the second in a series of public discussions on the world oil situation sponsored by the AEI National Energy Project. On our panel today are former Under Secretary of State George Ball; Canada's minister of energy, mines, and resources, Donald S. Macdonald; Sheikh Ahmed Zaki Yamani, minister of petroleum and mineral resources of Saudi Arabia; Senator Henry M. Jackson, chairman of the Senate interior committee; and John Sawhill, federal energy administrator. We will begin our discussion with a few opening remarks from each of the panelists. Then we will have a general discussion and will take some questions from the outstanding group of citizens in our audience. First, Mr. Ball.

GEORGE BALL, Lehman Brothers: The problem that the world faces today is the result of the increase in oil prices. The problem derives not so much from the fact of the increase as from the fact that it came so abruptly. If this increase in prices had taken place over a period of five or ten years, the problems of adjustment, I think, would have been manageable without extraordinary measures.

As it is, we are faced with a situation in which there are massive flows of capital into one area of the world, where, for a number of the countries that produce oil, the capacity to absorb this money and to use it internally does not exist. As a consequence, there are major dislocations in world financial markets which, in my judgment, require some extraordinary measures. And, in my opinion, the governments of the consuming nations have not faced this situation with any very great sense of reality.

I do, therefore, applaud the proposal that Dr. Witteveen, the president of the International Monetary Fund, is apparently putting forward for the creation of a facility in the monetary fund, but this measure alone seems to me to be quite inadequate. I think we need an approach that is very much more substantial than this. And perhaps in the course of this morning's discussion, I may have a chance to indicate my own views on that.

MR. LAIRD: Thank you, Mr. Ball. Minister Macdonald?

DONALD S. MACDONALD, Government of Canada: I think I would share the view of Mr. Ball with regard to the appropriateness, at least within a certain time frame, of moving toward higher energy prices. This was something that was bound to come about. Our view is that the era of cheap energy was clearly coming to an end in any event, and the decision of the OPEC countries really telescoped the time frame that was otherwise inevitable. It would, of course, have been desirable if this could have been achieved in a calmer atmosphere, one in which, for example, the world economy was not already dealing with difficulty with the problem of inflation. But the fact is, the time frame has been shortened, and it's with us now.

Probably the two fundamental questions in terms of meeting the problem are, first, the one that Mr. Ball has referred to—namely, the changing of international financial mechanisms to handle the balance-of-payments transfers that are involved—and second, with regard to both oil and many other commodities that originate in the developing countries, there is a great deal of importance in trying to determine what the real price of a commodity is and making certain, above all, that the developing countries share in the economic rent that should be available for most commodities.

MR. LAIRD: Thank you, Mr. Macdonald. Minister Yamani of Saudi Arabia.

SHEIKH AHMED ZAKI YAMANI, Government of Saudi Arabia: I think when we are discussing oil, we have two problems to face: number one, the price of oil, and number two, the availability of oil. Unfortunately, we are focusing nowadays only on the price of oil and forgetting in the meantime the main problem that the whole world will face very soon—the availability of oil.

I think because of the present surplus, which is a temporary thing, we forgot all about the so-called "energy crisis." And I think that we have to focus on that. I do support the views of Mr. Ball. I think regarding the price level, though it is on the high side, the problem is not the level of the price, it is the suddenness of the price increase, which created the surplus of money, a problem, in my opinion, that could be solved through various means, I don't think it is a very serious problem, if the oil-producing countries, the developing world, and the industrial world can sit down and discuss it.

MR. LAIRD: Thank you, Minister Yamani. Senator Jackson?

HENRY M. JACKSON, United States Senate (D-Wash.): Well, this problem, of course, is so involved and so all-pervasive, we could be here for weeks. There isn't anything that oil doesn't touch. We know what it is doing to the industrialized nations—Italy is on the edge of bankruptcy and we know what's happening in our own country.

In the less developed countries there is an obvious direct relationship between the price of oil and the availability of food. For example, the price and availability of oil determines the price and the availability of fertilizer. One billion people, almost one-quarter of the world's population, is fed by the extra crop yields that fertilizers produce.

For every pound of fertilizer that India lacks—just using India as an example —India loses ten pounds of wheat. This year's fertilizer shortage will cost India 10 million tons of grain, a year's supply for 50 million Indians.

I think it was Nobel Prize winner Norman Borlaug who estimated the other day that, with the price of petroleum products rising as it has been, 10 to 50 million people could starve in India this year alone.

In 1972, fertilizer prices averaged $150 per ton for nitrogen and phosphorus and $35.00 per ton for potassium, making the total cost of these nutrients to the less-developed countries about $525 million. Nineteen hundred and seventy-four prices will average $600 per ton for nitrogen and phosphorus and $100 per ton for potassium. Assuming the same quantities as for 1972, the 1974 cost will be $2 billion. That is, roughly, a 400 percent increase.

It is estimated that within the OPEC nations alone, there are 6.5 million barrels a day of idle productive capacity. I would like to propose to the leaders of OPEC that they dedicate, on humanitarian grounds, some portion of this capacity to the production of fertilizer for world peace and for the poor of the world. I propose that they sell this oil at its actual cost—ten to tweny cents per barrel— plus a nominal service charge of 15 to 20 percent. I wouldn't say this, except that the United States, I think, is in a position to say something about it. From 1946 through 1973 the less-developed countries of the world received from the United States of America, in the form of direct grants and gifts, $73 billion in economic assistance through Food for Peace and other aid programs. And when you take the developed countries to which we provided food and direct economic recon-struction aid after World War II, the total figure is $101 billion that we gave in the form of grants. Iran got from our country $2,128,000,000. I think it's now time for others, specifically OPEC members, to join in the effort to end starvation in the world by providing oil for fertilizer manufacture at cost or a small profit. The oil producers can now play, I think, a very important role in the cause of humanity. And I hope that some serious consideration will be given by the OPEC countries to achieve what I think is indeed a situation which in the next few months could border on catastrophe.

MR. LAIRD: Thank you Senator Jackson. Administrator John Sawhill.

MR. SAWHILL, Federal Energy Administration: First let me compliment you on having assembled such a panel with so many diversified interests and points of view. I think it is very healthy to have these kinds of discussions on such a critical problem.

From my perspective, it seems that the world's economy cannot withstand the very massive transfer of foreign exchange that is taking place today. Moreover, it seems to me that individual economies are having a difficult time operating in the uncertain atmosphere that is being engendered by the series of OPEC conferences and the threats of continued price increases that we are apparently facing.

The dilemma, I think, faces us because the international oil system has broken down. The international oil companies, which once served as a link between producing and consuming nations, can no longer guarantee stable supplies at reasonable and predictable prices. Now, I don't think it makes too much sense to try to point a finger at either side and say who is at fault. Rather, I think we need to seek solutions.

I would propose four things that the panel might consider: First, I believe the producing nations today are adding economics and politics to calculate oil prices, and from my perspective anyway, these two factors must be more carefully balanced in the future than they are today.

Second, since the U.S. oil companies are a major element in the oil supply system, our government has a special responsibility in establishing a new equilibrium between consuming and producing nations. We must consider ways to change and modify the relationships that we've established with the international oil companies in the past.

Third, I believe that consuming nations must work in concert, not to confront producing nations, but to cooperate in securing the mutual legitimate interests of both parties.

Fourth, since the U.S. consumes so much of the world's energy resources, I think we as Americans have a special responsibility to practice energy conservation. I strongly believe that America must show leadership in this area and take the lead in enacting at the federal level the measures which will show our own people as well as the people in the rest of the world that we are indeed serious about energy conservation.

And, finally, I believe that we have to remember that there is a human dimension to this problem, a dimension that's too often obscured, I believe, by impersonal geopolitical considerations. In the final analysis, as we sit here and discuss oil and oil availability and oil prices, we are really discussing the fate of human beings and the economic success or failure of those human beings. So I would just underscore the fact that this is a terribly important subject and one which we must begin quickly to find solutions for.

MR. LAIRD: Minister Yamani, the OPEC nations have called for a dialogue with the consuming nations and also the underdeveloped nations of the world. What progress has been made in that dialogue?

SHEIKH YAMANI: Before I deal with your question, Mr. Laird, I would like to respond to the advice given by Senator Jackson to the oil-producing countries. I would like to give him some information which might help to change that advice and find a better solution to the problem.

To start with, the reason why we have a very high price for fertilizers is, in our opinion and in the opinion of economists, the shortage in supply rather than the increase in oil prices. As we all know, the portion in the cost of producing fertilizer accounted for by oil is something between 20 and 25 percent. And this is not responsible for the 400 percent increase in fertilizer prices. There is now a shortage in the supply of fertilizer because of the closing down of some fertilizer plants in this and other countries. So, I think to face this problem, we'll have to build new fertilizer plants. Last April Saudi Arabia officially proposed in the United Nations to offer the abundant natural gas in Saudi Arabia. Of course, we cannot offer anything on behalf of Iran or Kuwait, but I'm sure that they have the same intentions in this area. We have an abundant amount of gas being flared nowadays. We want a global type of arrangement, and we are prepared to put the capital which we have into building enough fertilizer plants to feed the whole world.

It would seem rather illogical to use oil, which will be so valuable for the coming two decades at least, and leave aside the natural gas which we have now. I think the use of natural gas as a raw material is the solution to the problem, and the reason why the price of fertilizer is so high is definitely not a reflection of the price of oil as much as the scarcity, the shortage in the supply of fertilizer. And we have to do something about this.

I now want to express some of our views as oil producers. We see you as focusing too much on the price of oil, trying to tell your public in the Western world that this is *the* reason for inflation, which is not true. Inflation started well before we raised our price for oil. It is true that the high price of oil did contribute to the inflation rate, but the contribution is only 1 to 2 percent.

It is true that if we lower the price of oil, this will help reduce the inflation rate, but to a small extent. It is not true at all that by reducing the price of oil we will be able to fight and control inflation.

I think we have to be honest with ourselves, and I assure you that we in Saudi Arabia have an interest as producers in cooperating with you to fight inflation and control it. So let us look at the problem objectively and try to analyze it and face it with some courage. The surplus of money is a problem that could be solved through various means. I don't think it is a very serious one if we can sit down and discuss it among the oil-producing countries, the developing countries, and the major industrial countries. You have to help us industrialize our country, establish a substitute for the oil revenues which will go in the near future. We in Saudi Arabia have a development plan which will absorb in the coming five years not less than $60 billion.

Then, I think the developing world deserves real attention from all of us. And if we do this, we will help them to increase their purchasing power. We will help you in that. We do recognize the need to recycle this money in order to help the balance of payments in the world. We will be happy to sit down and discuss all of these problems together.

The Saudis have already proposed that a serious dialogue be initiated between the various parties concerned. We think that a committee representing, let's say, the oil producers, the industrial world, and the developing countries—a small committee of something like seven to eight nations, no more—can meet and set an agenda for these problems. I don't know how many issues there are right now, but I can say that oil, technology, raw materials, and recycling of money could be items on that agenda.

But talking about confrontation and headlines in the newspapers won't help anyone. It will hurt; it will create an atmosphere of hostility, and it will take us away from what we want. The problem that we are facing is not really a small one. Either we live or we don't live and I think we prefer the first choice.

MR. BALL: Much of what I have heard this morning I am in full accord with. I was particularly impressed with two comments that Mr. Sawhill made: that we should move toward cooperation with the OPEC countries to see if we can solve some of these problems together, and that the United States should take the lead in conservation measures.

I'm wholly in agreement with what he says, but I see very little evidence so far that the United States government, or indeed any other Western government with the possible exception of France, has done anything serious about this. As far as the question of cooperation is concerned, I think we've wasted a great deal of time in muttering and in conversations among the consuming nations about what might be done to bring pressure to lower the oil price. The time seems to me to be long overdue for us to get past this period of confrontation and have a dialogue with the producing nations, looking toward the solution of what has become a common problem, because the OPEC countries have as much interest as the industrial, consuming countries in not bringing about hardship to the less-developed countries and not disrupting the world financial mechanisms.

So I would certainly urge an effort to achieve a cooperative solution as soon as we can. And as far as the question of conservation is concerned, I would hope we'd do something about it. The fact is, as I say, that the French government has taken what seems to be a very useful measure. We've wasted months and nothing effective has been done so far as I can tell.

MR. MACDONALD: Well, I think that one can say that there have been international dialogues, but they have not been very fruitful. During the United Nations sessions last spring a number of extraneous political issues came up to obscure what is, after all, a substantial economic and political question.

I think a preparatory meeting of the kind suggested by Minister Yamani would be a very constructive initiative.

From the standpoint of my government, we find ourselves in the rather interesting situation of being both an exporter and a substantial importer of petroleum products. We would be delighted to participate in such a meeting. Also, I think that Senator Jackson's suggestion is also one of real interest. As the senator knows, Canada and the United States have been very heavy supporters of the World Food Program. And the suggestion, if I have it right, that the oil-producing states might contribute to the oil accounts of the less-developed countries in the way that we contributed to the World Food Program would at least cushion the impact of the price increase on some of those economies.

I would agree that the rest of us, the industrialized countries, should be prepared to pay our way in terms of oil prices, and in relation to our concerns, that is a recycling problem, as Mr. Ball has said, but I think the senator's initiative is one that we too would be interested in pursuing.

MR. LAIRD: Senator Jackson, we've heard discussion of conservation on the part of Mr. Sawhill and Mr. Ball. Why hasn't anything been done on conservation?

SENATOR JACKSON: Before I respond to your question, I want to commend Minister Yamani for his stated position. I think that he's been warning about the price of oil and the danger of a world depression, and I am aware of the initiatives taken by his government in connection with an adjustment in the price of oil.

We can talk all we want about doing something in the next four or five years. Everyone in America is beginning to understand that there is a direct relationship between the price of oil and what has been referred to by many as a situation in which we're on an edge of a financial panic. We're witnessing the greatest transfer of assets in the history of the world.

Now, there is no use beating around the bush. The sudden increase in the price of oil has impacted in a devastating way on all economies. For example, the other day West Germany provided $2 billion just to take care of the oil bill for Italy for the balance of this year, so that we are facing a catastrophic situation. So much for that. I just want to remind my fellow citizens that this nation has done its part in feeding the world to the tune of $100 billion, and I think the oil-producing countries now have a responsibility in this area that I hope they recognize soon.

On conservation, we passed an omnibus energy bill in the Senate and in the House, and the bill was vetoed. It provided authority for conservation measures. We have now passed out of my committee a bill that has been on the Senate calendar since April and that provides for stand-by authority for conservation measures, including rationing—which, with Mr. Laird, I believe is the sensible approach to this problem.

Now we need a signal—and we're waiting hopefully—that President Ford will change the position of the administration on this subject.

MR. LAIRD: Can't you change that position now, Mr. Sawhill?

SENATOR JACKSON: Can you make some news here, John? [Laughter.] If you can't, I understand Mr. Laird has a certain access to the White House. Maybe you could speak for the kitchen cabinet.

MR. LAIRD: Well, I think Mr. Sawhill can talk on that particular issue, because in the new administration—

SENATOR JACKSON: I noticed you two were whispering this morning.

MR. LAIRD: —departmental agencies are given greater responsibility, and with that responsibility comes the duty to speak out on some of these issues, too.

SENATOR JACKSON: I propose as a belt-tightening proposition that we follow the French lead, and have a "peril point" limiting the dollar amount we're going to permit to come into the country, and making up the difference by conservation and by stepped-up production, including the opening up of our petroleum reserves that are under the control of the navy. But the best thing that could happen is for the price of oil to drop $2.00 or $3.00 a barrel; otherwise we're talking about fictions, and not even good fictions.

On recycling, let's not kid the public. When you get through with it, Uncle Sam ends up with all the funny money—all of the IOUs. And the course here is so clear that it seems to me that we ought to be honest about it. If the price of oil does not come down in the next few months even by $2.00 or $3.00 a barrel, the financial situation in Western Europe, Japan, North America, and the under-developed world is going to be disastrous.

Let's face this candidly. It's a problem of educating our own people. I think we have to explain to them that we're sitting on a time bomb. All of our investment in saving the economies of Western Europe and Japan after World War II will go down the drain, sure as I'm sitting in this chair, unless something changes. If someone's got a formula that shows a different picture with oil prices staying at the present level I'd like to know about it.

We can talk conservation; we can save 2 million barrels a day out of our 17 million average daily consumption and when you're through, the United States can survive, but what happens to the other countries?

88

MR. LAIRD: Secretary Ball?

MR. BALL: I must say that I share Senator Jackson's very deep concern about the future, if we continue as we now are. I would suggest, however, that if the price of oil is to come down, it is most likely to be in response to a reduction in demand. And that, in turn, requires conservation measures on the part of the United States and all other consuming countries. Therefore, I put a top priority on moving to very serious, quite stringent conservation measures.

Now, as far as the less-developed countries are concerned, there is no question in my mind that they are in very serious condition and that any capital flow to them has got to be very heavily subsidized. It has got to be subsidized by the OPEC countries, and I would assume that it must be on some kind of a sharing basis with the industrialized consuming countries as well. There are mechanisms that can be set up for this.

As far as countries such as Italy are concerned, they are bearing a very heavy burden at this time, and it will take time and a strong political will for them to do the things at home that will be necessary in order to be able to absorb these increased energy costs. In the meantime, they need help as well. And here again, I hope that the burden is one that will be borne equally by the U.S., Europe and the OPEC countries. For this reason, it seems to me some kind of an international mechanism in which the OPEC countries fully share is essential. But this can only be brought about by a serious dialogue between the producers and the consumers.

MR. MACDONALD: What is the best way to get that dialogue going?

MR. BALL: I would suggest that we have a discussion between representatives of the OPEC countries and of the consuming countries, and that we talk quite frankly about the problem of the less-developed countries.

SENATOR JACKSON: I wonder if we can clarify one thing: you mentioned that by cutting demand we are going to fix a just price. I don't believe that. This is the most efficient cartel in the world. Now, my point is very simple: The OPEC countries are reducing production. They are in a position to say, "Well, look, if demand goes down, we'll go down on production." Demand is down, worldwide. But what has happened to price? Price is up.

MR. SAWHILL: Well, I think the point is not that price necessarily will go down if demand goes down, but the only alternative we really have to try to get the price down is for the United States and the world to begin practicing conservation.

SENATOR JACKSON: I buy that completely. But all I'm saying is we're not talking about a free market. It is a cartel market.

MR. BALL: I wholly agree with Senator Jackson. I wholly agree that it's not a market that is immediately responsive to market forces, and it's not likely to be disrupted immediately by market forces. I think over the long term, perhaps, it may.

MR. SAWHILL: The larger the gap, though, between productive capacity and actual production, the greater the opportunity for a cartel to begin to disintegrate to some extent, and, therefore, for prices to begin to come down.

SENATOR JACKSON: But why would a country—and I have great respect for Minister Yamani—why would countries like Saudi Arabia, Abu Dhabi, Libya and others not hesitate to cut back production when they don't need any more money? They can meet all of their needs by the end of this year with what they are currently accumulating. There are two countries in OPEC that have a special problem—Iran and Venezuela—because of their huge development programs. But where is the incentive for others not to cut back production?

MR. SAWHILL: I think probably we ought to ask Mr. Yamani to comment, but first I might just add that not every country is in the fortunate position of Saudi Arabia. Many of these countries need these funds for their own internal develop-ment. So it's not entirely clear that every country can participate in a continuing cutback as the consuming world begins practicing conservation.

SHEIKH YAMANI: I want you to know that I will be happy if you succeed in this conservation program, not because it will bring price down, but because it will help us conserve the available oil for the remaining part of this century. If we have an increase in demand of 2 to 3 percent annually, I think the oil we have all over the world will only be enough for twenty-five years. So we always feel happy when we see countries like the United States and France really trying to cut demand. I think that if we reduce the price of oil a little bit this will help the balance of payments in the world, but again, I want to repeat, it won't help inflation.

Now, back to OPEC and level of production. Some of the OPEC countries are really reducing their production, but in very insignificant amounts. The countries who can affect the supply picture significantly, such as Iran and Saudi Arabia, are not cutting production.

Here is where I disagree with Mr. Sawhill: I don't think that OPEC will disintegrate, because the margin between our full production capacity and what we need to produce to live well is so huge. What we are doing right now is some-thing foolish, if viewed from the narrow angle of our selfish interest in Saudi Arabia. We are producing 5.5 million barrels a day just to help the economy of the world, to help hold off another price increase.

I think that conservation alone will never put a real downward pressure on the price of oil. There should be another avenue for you to take, and that's a meeting with the producers. I think the oil producers won't sit down to a discussion with only the oil consumers. They will want to talk with the less-developed countries, too. I don't foresee that we will be able to solve everything overnight. I think we'll do it step by step, but it has to be done under one umbrella.

SENATOR JACKSON: Mr. Minister, I believe you are to be commended for at times taking a dissenting view in the OPEC community. I think with your broad training and experience, you have a keen understanding of the dangers that exist in this situation.

I agree with your suggestion of sitting down and talking with the OPEC countries. There have been general discussions, but could you outline something that will be more specific so that we can have some meaningful discussions?

Recently one of our cabinet officials said he thought the price of oil would be coming down $2.00 a barrel—there was to be an oil auction by your country—and there were big headlines in our papers "Oil is Coming Down"—and the stock market shot up for a few days. Then there was a big letdown.

SHEIKH YAMANI: I think the price of oil did go down. What you have to consider is the market price. The market price sometime in January went up to $17.00 per barrel, f.o.b. the Gulf.

SENATOR JACKSON: Some of it went as high as $24.00 on spot sales over here during the embargo.

SHEIKH YAMANI: And even after the embargo the price of oil was something like $12.00 to $13.00 per barrel. Now it went down to something less than $10.00. This is due, on one side, to the decrease in demand, and, on the other side, to a lack of response to that drop in demand by some of the exporting countries, mainly Saudi Arabia. So the price of oil went down, and I hope it will continue to go down, but in a very quiet manner—with fewer headlines.

SENATOR JACKSON: How would it be at that point if I suggested to the President that we take the initiative? I sponsored a bill that was passed but vetoed, which would have provided that on "new oil" in the United States the average price would be about $7.90 a barrel. All of our experts say there is no relationship between the price increase in our country and new oil. In fact, production is going down in the United States. We're getting new oil rigs, but production is going down.

How would you feel about that kind of an initiative here? It would involve about 40 percent of our production, which is now unregulated and is at the world cartel price.

MR. SAWHILL: Let me chime in here to say that the average price in this country is still considerably below the world price and the Canadian price.

SENATOR JACKSON: Yes, the average price, but the authority to hold "old oil" at $5.25 a barrel expires February 28. And I'm not so sure that the old oil is being pumped out as fast as it could be, because I think a lot of the companies are sitting on it, hoping that the price will double.

SHEIKH YAMANI: I really don't think that anything will cause a reduction in world prices unless you reduce the price in the Gulf, which is the main source of supply. What you are suggesting will not change things there.

Go back a few years to when you had a very high price on indigenous United States oil, which was almost double the price of what you imported from us.

SENATOR JACKSON: Yes, but what is the difference in cost of production? Five cents a barrel over there versus $2.40 over here.

SHEIKH YAMANI: Cost of production has nothing to do with your price of oil. Your domestic oil price was almost double the price of imported oil, and we couldn't increase our prices. The same will be true in reverse under your proposal. I am afraid that you would discourage further exploration in this country. I think you have to help the private sector to invest in this area and explore for more oil.

I am really very sincere in this opinion, though it might appear as if I am working against our interests. I look at it for the long term, and I know for sure that what you are discussing today will be history maybe in one or two years. I think when we are discussing oil, we do have two problems to face—number one, the price of oil, and number two, the availability of oil. Unfortunately, we are focusing nowadays only on the price of oil and forgetting for a while the main problem the whole world will face very soon: the availability of oil.

MR. SAWHILL: Well, I think it is a question of the short range and the long range. In the short run I honestly believe that the real problem is the price. Senator Jackson has said we are facing a financial crisis.

SENATOR JACKSON: No, that was David Rockefeller. *He* said a financial "panic."

MR. SAWHILL: I gathered you agreed with him when you quoted him.

SENATOR JACKSON: Well, I don't know— [Laughter.]

MR. SAWHILL: Well, anyway, Mr. Ball has suggested that we are facing a serious financial situation if we cannot get a mechanism going to recycle these billions of dollars in excess funds that are building up in the OPEC nations. Frankly, I agree with that, because annual OPEC revenues have gone from some $20 billion to over

$100 billion in a very short—two-year—period. I don't think the world's economic institutions can provide that kind of recycling mechanism, so while I agree with Minister Yamani that the long-run problem is supply and we have got to take major initiatives all over the world to bring on new sources of energy, it seems to me the short-run problem is how the world's economic systems can survive this very rapid run up in price. That is why we are focusing so much on price.

SHEIKH YAMANI: You will be irresponsible in this country if you don't work very hard to find some additional sources of energy, whether it is oil, coal, atomic— whatever it is. I think you will be responsible, and everybody is responsible in this country for it. We also feel responsible, though we are far away from the problem. But since we have the huge reserve, we think that you should share the burden with us.

I want you to adjust yourself to the new economic reality that there is a transfer of wealth from the industrial world to a group of developing nations, the oil-producing nations. You cannot do anything about that by saying, "We don't want it. We have to stop it. We have to reduce the oil price; we have to do this and that. You have to recycle the money the way we want it."

I think such an approach is very unhealthy, and you won't solve the problem this way. What you have to do is sit down with the new wealthy group of people, if you can call them this, and see how you can meet their requirements and how you can solve your problem. They are ready to sit down with you and they are ready to cooperate and help. You have to accept this new reality that a group of producers like Iran, Saudi Arabia, the other Arab nations, and Venezuela are becoming wealthy and they want to utilize their new wealth in cooperation with you.

MR. LAIRD: Thank you very much. Now, we'll have questions from our guests in the audience.

ARDESHIR ZAHEDI, Government of Iran: Let me tell you how happy I am to take part in such a wide-ranging discussion as this. As I said yesterday, I don't believe we can get anywhere by confrontation or gunboat diplomacy, and so I am happy and optimistic now that we are taking real steps toward a serious dialogue.

In the last few months we have often heard that it is the oil-producing countries who are responsible for this problem. I do not agree with this. Before the October War, the problem of inflation had nothing to do with the price of oil.

I believe the OPEC countries have said many, many times that they are willing and they would like to cooperate in dealing with the world economic problem.

MR. LAIRD: Your question goes to that point? I'm trying to get the question, so we can direct it to one of our panel members.

SENATOR JACKSON: I wonder if we could get to the real point here. I don't know what is happening, but they tell me that by next July 1 the OPEC countries will have more foreign exchange than all of the industrialized nations put together. What is happening?

AMBASSADOR ZAHEDI: When I was working in Point Four, we used to buy sugar for my country at $35.00 per ton. Today you have to pay $800 and something for it. I can tell you one thing very honestly: if you think the price of oil is going to come down to $4.00 or $5.00 a barrel, you won't get it.

SENATOR JACKSON: The argument that other commodities have gone up has been used over and over. Let me just give you the specific figures: The Conference Board, on the basis of United Nations International Monetary Fund data, shows that since 1963 the world export price of oil has climbed 636 percent compared to about 290 percent for nonferrous metals, 230 percent for crude oil, and 175 percent for manufacturing.

What I want to know is what you are going to do about your brethren in the Third World, who are facing possible starvation, now that you have got all of this money?

MR. LAIRD: I think that this particular question is very important, and I would like to have a response from Minister Yamani.

SHEIKH YAMANI: Now, I have to talk on behalf of Saudi Arabia. Saudi Arabia allocated 10 percent of its national budget this year for foreign aid. We have a responsibility and you have a responsibility. We both—the industrial world and the oil-producing countries—have to help and contribute to the starving peoples in the developing countries.

Now, coming back to the price of oil, I want to say that the price of a barrel of crude in 1947 was higher than the price of that barrel of crude in 1970. There is no other commodity on earth whose price has been so depressed.

But you do have the right to complain of the sudden, high increase of prices. And we are ready to sit down and discuss it and see how we can solve the problem.

AMBASSADOR ZAHEDI: First of all, I would like to say that we do appreciate what your country has done, Senator Jackson. In the last ten or fifteen years you have helped us to the tune of almost $2.5 billion.

Now, we are trying to help. We have a population of only 32 million, and this year we have already committed ourselves to more than $8 billion in aid. This $8 billion is not only going to Italy, France, and England, which are developed countries, but also to India, Egypt, and other countries.

JOHN NASSIKAS, Federal Power Commission: I would like to direct this question, if I may, to Mr. Yamani. You mentioned the conversion of some of your flared gas resources to the manufacture of fertilizer. I seriously doubt that there is enough gas being flared in the world to handle the world's fertilizer needs. Do you not think that there must be sources of fertilizer other than natural gas? Everytime we export food and fertilizer from the United States, we are of course exporting natural gas, which is in very short supply. So I applaud your objective. It is just that I don't know whether it can be realized.

SHEIKH YAMANI: I think my goal can be realized. The problem is not the availability of natural gas. The problem is the possibility of producing more fertilizer than the world needs. If we do this, we hurt ourselves. What we need is a global meeting of all the parties concerned so we can produce exactly what is needed and so we can work out some sort of settlement for the debts that will be incurred. As you know, a good number of the consumers will not have enough money to pay for fertilizer.

GEORGE LENCZOWSKI, University of California: There has been much discussion about the price of oil—and this is understandable, because price is the current and major problem. But I remember that Minister Yamani at the beginning of his remarks mentioned that there are two problems: price and availability.

I would like to address myself to the second problem and link it with the general political circumstances which have surrounded the availability of oil. There was an interruption of oil supplies last year because of political reasons. I wonder, Sheikh Yamani, whether you would make any comments on the further availability of oil in connection with the political situation, and whether the price of oil, as some newspapers have asserted, is in any way, in the Arab eyes, linked to the international political situation, particularly the Middle East conflict.

SHEIKH YAMANI: I think, even without any political interruption, the oil available to us is not enough. We have to work very hard to establish substitutes and to try to find more oil. As for the latter, Saudi Arabia has the best potential in the whole world. If we try very hard to find oil in Saudi Arabia and elsewhere, maybe we'll be able to meet world demands until the end of this century.

As for the political element, I think the Saudis have made it very clear that they hate to use oil as a weapon, and I think all the other producers in the Arab world are not fond of doing this. But we do have a problem, and that problem is still with us. The problem is the Palestinian issue and the occupation of our territory. These ingredients caused the October War last year. If we don't solve these issues, there will be another war. And there will be another interruption in the supply of oil. Let us both work very hard to save humanity from this problem.

Now I come to the last point you mentioned, the political link to the price of oil. As we all know, the oil producers are not all Arabs. Oil comes from Venezuela, Iran, Indonesia, Nigeria, Gabon, Ecuador, and other places. We cannot say that if you solve our political problem, we guarantee that the price of oil will go down. But I can see that the Arabs will definitely compete more and more if they get peace in their area. This means that the price of oil will go down, because the Arab producers are really the largest producers.

CHARLES H. MURPHY, JR., Murphy Oil Corporation: The profits Senator Jackson keeps talking about are not only obscene, they are illusory because they don't exist in treasury cash. They are largely tied up in inventory and accounts receivable.

Senator Jackson, do you have in mind any measures that would speed up the process of capital formation and the commitment of that capital to the development of our indigenous resources in America?

SENATOR JACKSON: It has been argued that there should be no price ceiling on new oil so that new discoveries of oil would be stimulated. As you know, Mr. Murphy, it just hasn't worked out that way. In fact, I read in the paper that the second or third largest oil company found that it had such a huge cash flow that it decided to buy Montgomery Ward, the corporate holding company being Marco. Now, how do you explain that to the American people? How can you expect them to believe that you're not making enough money to do the development work?

Obviously, that isn't the issue, and that isn't the problem. I want to see a fair price. I suggest $7.09 a barrel, which is $2.00 above what the industry association said was necessary as a target price to provide the incentive to get new oil. In any case, the problem is a shortage of equipment, and that is the problem the bill gave the President the authority to deal with by issuing priorities to get the drilling equipment and the steel.

I would like for you to explain to the public why the production of oil is going down continuously in the United States.

MR. SAWHILL: Maybe I could add a footnote to Senator Jackson's answer, since he and I sometimes disagree.

It is true that the production of oil is going down in the United States. As a matter of fact, our figures show that production will probably continue to decline through 1977, because we are continuing to experience very sharp declines in our existing oil fields.

Nevertheless, drilling activity is now 30 percent above what it was at this time last year, which, I believe, augurs very well for the future and indicates that the current new oil price is serving as an incentive to bring on new supply.

SENATOR JACKSON: Why, then, is Mobil going out and buying Montgomery Ward at a price of $800 million?

SHEIKH YAMANI: I think this so-called windfall profit for the oil companies is derived from the production outside the United States, and it's due to the difference—the gap—between the average cost for the oil companies and market price, and to a great extent to the inventory.

SALEM AL-SABAH, Government of Kuwait: There are two points I want to touch on and then I'll direct a question to Senator Jackson.

My country is an oil-producing country. We cut our production simply because we want to prolong the reserves of our oil, which guarantee a better future for our coming generations. These are all we have, so we must be very careful with them.

Also, Kuwait believes in doing her part in international society. I agree with the senator that we have to pay great attention to the developing countries and the countries which suffer from the rise of price of not only oil but other materials. As Sheikh Yamani said, and Kuwait believes, since we went to the United Nations last year for that particular purpose, why don't we sit together and find a settlement for all prices for all materials and commodities? Also, Kuwait has established the Kuwait Development Fund, to which it has devoted 10 percent of its national income—$12 billion this year alone.

And now the question: Instead of having confrontations, why don't the United States, Kuwait, Saudi Arabia, and other OPEC members sit together and try to find ways to develop Third World nations?

SENATOR JACKSON: Well, Mr. Ambassador, as has been mentioned here, there's a great transfer of wealth going on. The OPEC countries will have more foreign exchange than the United States and all Western industrialized nations put together by next July 1. Maybe you could help undertake to feed the developing countries and relieve us of that burden. We're going to have to pick up all of the "funny money."

AMBASSADOR AL-SABAH: We don't want to give charity; we want to give aid.

HENDRIK HOUTHAKKER, Harvard University: I would like to address a question to Senator Jackson. This goes back to the very valuable suggestions made by Minister Yamani concerning U.S. policy. In particular, Minister Yamani emphasized the importance of oil production, and I would like to underscore this. I believe that more production in the long run is a better road to lower prices than conservation, even though conservation may be necessary in the short run. And I would like to add parenthetically that rationing doesn't strike me as the right approach at all. Now then, we have seen declines in U.S. production, and Mr. Sawhill has just said that he expects them to continue. Don't you think, Senator, that these declines are due in large part to the distinction between old oil and new oil in existing legislation? This distinction really discourages more production from existing fields. I believe that we would be better off having a single price for oil.

SENATOR JACKSON: Well, Professor, as you know, the decision on a ceiling on old oil was not made by the Congress, it was made pursuant to the authority granted under the Mandatory Fuel Allocations Act. And an arbitrary increase of about $1.00 a barrel to $5.25 a barrel was worked out by the administration.

I want to point out that the key problem on more oil—and this is the crux of the debate—is not price; it's a shortage of oil rigs. Should we continue doing what we did in the twelve months up to June 30 of this year? The Export-Import Bank granted loans for oil rigs to go abroad to the tune of about $500 million and up to February 1 the interest rate was 6 percent and after February 1 was 7 percent.

The problem is the fact that we do not have authority—because it was vetoed— to provide for a proper, mandatory allocation of the critical materials needed for oil drilling. And we are allowing those critical materials to be used for all sorts of speculative purposes.

MR. SAWHILL: I was almost going to agree with Senator Jackson until he got on the mandatory allocation question. But it seems to me that I have to take responsibility for the two-tier price system. I do not think that two-tier price system is restricting production. I do not think that if we eliminated the two-tier price system our projections for oil supplies over the next two to three years would change one bit. The thing that is restricting our oil supplies is the availability, as Senator Jackson points out, of drilling rigs and tubular steel. And in contrast with what Senator Jackson said, I should point out that we have invoked the Defense Production Act to make critical materials available to the Alaska Pipeline to ensure that we get that oil as quickly as possible.

HERBERT STEIN, University of Virginia: I would like to ask Minister Yamani if he would say a few words about the principles which in his mind determine the OPEC oil-price policy. Why is the price not $20.00 a barrel, why is it not $5.00 a barrel? More specifically, is he concerned with the possibility that at something like the present price of oil, there may be such an enormous investment on the part of the rest of the world in developing alternative sources of energy and developing adaptations of living without energy, that in the end Saudi Arabians and others may find, one or two generations from now, that they are left with a large pool of oil which is less valuable than they now expect it will be?

SHEIKH YAMANI: I have now to disclose our internal problems. I don't think we do agree inside OPEC on what the price should be. We do have member countries who think it should go up right now to something like $15.00 or $17.00 per barrel of crude.

There are also countries like Saudi Arabia who think it should go below the present level. And there are countries who would accept at the end of the argument—and I assure you it is a very hot argument—a freeze in the posted price of oil.

I am afraid there is no real principle as such in OPEC. As an economist you will tell me that the law of supply and demand will work. It has worked, so far. The market price went down a little bit. It went up sharply because of the oil embargo; when again we had a normal situation sometime in May or June, it went down. It went down further because of the surplus in the market, which was not entirely taken care of by the reduction in production. What will happen in the future is unknown. But, definitely, the law of supply and demand does work right now.

I disagree with Senator Jackson's view that we have a strong cartel. Unless you have Saudi Arabia contributing to that cartel, the cartel will not be strong. Unless Iran cooperates—cutting down 2 million barrels, which they can do—there won't be a strong cartel.

SENATOR JACKSON: We understood that you were going to have an oil auction. Now that would test the market. Can you give us some assurance that you will go through with an auction in the future? Right now you are candidly admitting that the price is being fixed.

SHEIKH YAMANI: I don't think that an oil auction as such can be a main factor in determining prices. The main factor is the oil we have to sell in the market.

We do have an arrangement which we are discussing with the oil companies. What the arrangement will be and how much oil we will have in our hands and how we are going to sell it—whether through auction, or through direct negotiations— that is another thing. The market will decide on that whenever we have the oil.

But we have not yet finished the arrangements with the oil companies. Once we do, we will sell our oil, and the law of supply and demand will define the price of the oil, whether through negotiations, or through auction.

MR. SAWHILL: Sheikh Yamani, earlier we talked about conservation. If the United States and the rest of the world were able through conservation to cut their demand back by some 3 million barrels a day—which is perhaps optimistic, but it could be done—what do you think would happen to price?

SHEIKH YAMANI: It would go down.

MR. SAWHILL: Thank you very much.

SHEIKH YAMANI: I think if you do this it will go down, unless some of the major producers cut their production drastically. Now the number one producer that can do this is Saudi Arabia, and I can tell you right now, we won't cut down our production.

MR. SAWHILL: Great. Thank you very much. [Applause.] You have just given a ringing endorsement for a conservation program in the consuming nations, and I certainly do appreciate that.

SHEIKH YAMANI: But definitely, if we raise our oil price by something like 20 to 25 percent, I don't think we will need to have alternative sources of energy; we will have a disaster all over the world.

SENATOR JACKSON: Mr. Chairman, I have to leave—

MR. LAIRD: Senator Jackson is going to try to answer a roll call on the floor of the Senate.

SENATOR JACKSON: We have been in session since nine o'clock and I have been playing "hookey." But I want to say to Minister Yamani that, while we may disagree on some things, I think his participation here this morning has been very useful. I hope there will be more of this, because I think the problem is too serious to permit communications to break down.

CHARLES SPAHR, Standard Oil of Ohio: I would like to address my question to Minister Yamani. Is Saudi Arabia willing to invest some substantial part of its funds in nitrogen chemical fertilizer plants, without partners, at its sole risk? If so, what rate of return would have to be envisioned to trigger that kind of an investment?

SHEIKH YAMANI: Well, it should be inside Saudi Arabia, utilizing our own natural gas. We are now embarking on a very ambitious fertilizer program in Saudi Arabia—petrochemical industry as well as fertilizers. We are willing to put up as much capital as is needed, but we definitely need your technology, and we need your markets. It is a policy of the Saudi government to have some foreign capital— not because we need it, but because we need your sincere efforts. This might differ from the policies in some other countries where they want to dominate everything, and where they have some inhibition against any foreign capital. We don't have such inhibitions. We believe in this type of relationship. Now the capital is not a problem. But all that we need is to create an interest for you in Saudi Arabia.

MR. SPAHR: And the rate of return?

SHEIKH YAMANI: Well, it should be a reasonable rate of return. I would say the rate of return needed to proceed is from 10 to 15 percent—something reasonable.

REZA FALLAH, Iranian National Oil Company: Thank you. Had there been more time I would like to comment on that, on the basic issue raised on the panel. But that I should have to skip at the moment. There are two remarks I must make.

The main theme of this conference has been lowering the price of oil. My question in response has always been, "What price?" It is surprising that when we get a gathering of so many experts, and we talk about reducing the price, we don't know what price that we are talking about. In my country I am in charge of that particular department, and if you ask me what is the price of oil, I will give you one, two, three, or four different prices.

We have a basic price, which Mr. Yamani knows. If he succeeds in his deal with ARAMCO, his public will have a basic price. That basic price is not high; it is low. At the moment it is not more than, perhaps, $8.40 in the marketplace. Then there are other prices—"buy backs," and various others—that come into the picture and inflate the price that the customer pays. One day I think we shall have to sit down together and try and find out what we are talking about.

MR. SAWHILL: I couldn't agree more that there is confusion as to what the world oil price is. We talk about "equity" oil, and "buyback" oil, and "posted" price, and "tax-paid" cost. Frankly, I think we confuse people all over the world. I know that your country and Sheikh Yamani's have both expressed many times the need to move toward a single price for oil, and I think we can see around the world that the concession system is undergoing a substantial amount of change, and probably will eventually end.

With the demise of the concession system, there is going to come a single price, which is going to make it much easier for us to communicate and to know exactly what price we are talking about. Fundamentally what we are talking about is lowering the cost of oil to consuming nations because it has gone up so steeply. Again, I think Sheikh Yamani made a very good point when he said very directly and clearly, that there has been and will continue to be a transfer of wealth. This is not going to change, and the laws of supply and demand are not going to be repealed in that way.

But it is this very rapid increase in price that I agree has got to result in some kind of a cooperative solution, whether it is in a meeting or in individual negotiations. Clearly, one of the results of these negotiations has got to be agreement on some kind of simpler pricing system. It is much too confusing today.

DR. FALLAH: Anyway, the price of just over $8.00 is a low price. That, as I suggested yesterday, can never be reduced. But around that, I think we need to discuss ways and means of trying to find a solution equitable to both sides.

Oil is subject to supply and demand. Maybe it is off your point, but whereas most commodities are replaceable year after year, oil is not. So another factor comes into oil pricing, and that is the replacement value. When we have finished our resources, we have got to buy back the same energy—very likely from the West. We have got to pay not more than what we received from you. So this is an item which must be taken into consideration.

Finally, let me say that there are three prime architects of this energy crisis: governments of the producing countries, governments of the consuming countries, and the intermediary oil companies.

In the past, the oil companies have been to blame. They didn't see the writing on the wall that they should put up the price because it was very low—for decades. When they had the prerogative of increasing prices I think they should have done so, but they missed the boat. Prices went down, imports went up, and naturally, there was a reaction from the producers: the prices went up; there was a price explosion.

The oil companies also neglected to develop alternative sources and build enough refining capacity in the consuming countries.

I'm sorry to say the consuming governments turned a deaf ear to indications by OPEC that they would like to have a round table conference on the question. Nothing was done. Instead, communications have been issued which have had militant tones at times. They haven't been friendly; there was the threat of confrontation. Altogether they have produced some sort of a crusade, which to my mind has done a great deal of harm. If some of the politicians—I won't mention names—cannot remain within diplomatic language, they should observe the bounds of politeness, which they don't. That already is costing the consumer, because it certainly drives the producer into the corner.

Now, as far as OPEC is concerned, if they follow the lead by Iran and Saudi Arabia and come to a single pricing system, then that will eliminate the confusion which is reigning at the moment.

ELVIS J. STAHR, National Audubon Society: The need for conservation has been stressed and reiterated this morning. I am very happy about that, for it seems to me that the biggest obstacle to a really significant energy conservation program, at least in this country, is a persistent public lack of awareness of the need for it.

I am very happy that a number of the needs and a number of the benefits of conservation have been brought out today. There are many: reducing the pressures on our environment, reducing air and water pollution, reducing pressure on interest rates, reducing the enormous capital needs for investment by utilities and extractive industries if there is a continuing growth in demand for greater and greater supply, and more. There are so many benefits that accrue from conservation that I hope we approach it not just as something that we have to do because the world oil crises suddenly jumped up on us.

MR. LAIRD: I think this is a fine way to end our meeting today. Thank you all. [Applause.]

CONFERENCE PARTICIPANTS

Al-Sabah, Salem, *Kuwaiti Ambassador to the United States*

Anthony, John, *School for Advanced International Studies, Johns Hopkins University*

Aragon, Manuel, *Deputy Mayor, Los Angeles, California*

Ball, George W., *Senior Partner, Lehman Brothers*

Baroody, William J., *President, American Enterprise Institute*

Cadieux, Marcel, *Canadian Ambassador to the United States*

Campbell, W. Glenn, *Director, Hoover Institution, Stanford*

Fallah, Reza, *Director of International Affairs, National Iranian Oil Company*

Greenspan, Alan, *Chairman, Council of Economic Advisers*

Houthakker, Hendrik, *Professor of Economics, Harvard University*

Ignatius, Paul R., *President, Air Transport Association*

Jackson, Henry M., *United States Senator, Washington*

Laird, Melvin R., *Chairman, American Enterprise Institute's National Energy Project*

Lenczowski, George, *Professor of Political Science, University of California, Berkeley*

Levy, Walter, *Walter Levy and Associates*

Lichtblau, John, *Executive Director, Petroleum Industry Research Foundation, Inc.*

Loftness, Robert, *Director of the Washington Office, Electric Power Research Institute*

Macdonald, Donald, *Minister, Department of Energy, Mines and Resources, Canada*

Mitchell, Edward J., *Director, American Enterprise Institute's National Energy Project*

Murphree, Gwen, *Chairman, League of Women Voters Education Fund's Energy Task Force*

Murphy, Charles H., Jr., *Chairman of the Board, Murphy Oil Corporation*

Nassikas, John, *Chairman, Federal Power Commission*

Osment, Frank, *Executive Vice President, Standard Oil of Indiana*

Piercy, George, *Director and Senior Vice President, Exxon Corporation*

Pranger, Robert J., *Director of Foreign and Defense Policy Studies, American Enterprise Institute*

Royster, Vermont, *William R. Kenan, Jr., Professor of Journalism and Public Affairs at the University of North Carolina*

Ruppe, Philip, *United States Congressman, Michigan*

Sawhill, John C., *Administrator, Federal Energy Administration*

Spahr, Charles E., *Chairman, Standard Oil of Ohio*

Stahr, Elvis J., *President, National Audubon Society*

Stein, Herbert, *A. Willis Robertson Professor of Economics, University of Virginia*

Yamani, Sheikh Ahmed Zaki, *Minister of Petroleum and Mineral Resources, Saudi Arabia*

Zahedi, Ardeshir, *Iranian Ambassador to the United States*